Using National Standards to Improve Performance

James Holyfield
and
Karen Moloney

This book is dedicated to all those who have made
Standards and NVQs work.

First published in 1996

Kogan Page Limited
120 Pentonville Road
London N1 9JN

© James Holyfield and Karen Moloney, 1996

British Library Cataloguing in Publication Data

A CIP record for this book is available from the British Library.

ISBN 0 7494 1872 9

Typeset by Northern Phototypesetting, Co Ltd, Bolton
Printed and bound in Great Britain by Biddles Ltd, Guildford and King's Lynn

CONTENTS

ACKNOWLEDGEMENTS

The authors of this book would like to thank the following for their co-operation and help: Elizabeth Rylance Watson (NVQ Development Officer, British Council); Carol Smalley (Post Office Pensions Administration, Chesterfield); Christine Webb (PMI); Carolyn Mason and Tony Miles (Glaxo-Wellcome, Dartford); and all those people who have kept us up to date with developments in the field, especially: Peter Armstrong; Colin Lees; Andy Wallis; Ken Richardson (BP Chemicals Ltd); Barry Howells (SCM Chemicals).

With special thanks to colleagues at the Chemical Industries Association and Moloney & Gealy: Anna Benjamin (M&G); Lindsey Brown (M&G); Denise Clark (M&G); Martin Draper (M&G); Jim Foulds (CIA); Norman Gealy (M&G); Sonia Harris (M&G); Pauline Haste (M&G); Douglas MacDonald (M&G); Bill McNichol (CIA); Teresa Neale (CIA); and Debra Westlake (M&G).

Crown copyright is reproduced with the permission of the Controller of HMSO.

FOREWORD

The idea of a clear and comprehensive system of occupational standards and qualifications is a good one. It makes a lot of sense and can bring tremendous benefits for employers and employees alike.

It is astonishing that there are numbers of people who still receive no training throughout their working lives. Others, because of the lack of a training culture in British organisations, still consider training as something which is done to them, rather than something which can actively assist their career and personal development.

This book says quite simply that we cannot and need not go on like this. Through the national standards and qualifications programme, a number of tools have been developed which can help organisations to improve their performance. These tools are free; they will cost you nothing. They are effective and easy to use. And they can bring business benefits which it could be unwise to ignore.

The standards and qualifications programme has been criticised on the grounds of complexity. It can be difficult, it does take effort; but where people are concerned, the effort is justified.

Glenda Jackson MP

INTRODUCTION

WHAT'S IT ALL ABOUT?

First, some definitions. This book is about national standards and vocational qualifications.

If you haven't already come across them, national standards are published descriptions of the performance expected of someone who is competent in an occupation. So, for example, there is a set of standards for bricklayers, which describes the functions of a bricklayer, the quality and scope of work expected of a competent bricklayer, and the criteria by which you would judge the work of a bricklayer. Similarly, there are standards for accountants, bus drivers, company directors, and just about every other occupation in Britain – with other countries such as New Zealand, South Africa and Australia following suit.

To support the development of competence throughout the British workforce, vocational qualifications are being developed which measure and confirm that someone is meeting the national standards. These vocational qualifications are unlike any other. They measure competence, and they measure it in the work environment.

NVQs are National Vocational Qualifications, SVQs are Scottish Vocational Qualifications. NVQs and SVQs are vocational qualifications of the new type. They have been accredited by NCVQ (The National Council for Vocational Qualifications) and SCOTVEC (The Scottish Vocational Education Council) as confirmation that their holders can meet the relevant national standards.

WHY THIS BOOK?

We decided to write this book for two reasons. First, we believe that national standards and qualifications present an outstanding opportunity for British business that we feel should not be missed. Second, we fear that many people have been wrongly informed about national standards and NVQs/SVQs and we want to present the facts.

We have been unashamedly biased. We believe that national standards and the qualifications derived from them are not only the biggest revolution in the vocational education and training sector in Britain for decades, but they are an innovative vehicle for change in the way we handle people in organisations.

They are having an impact on human resource development in this country equivalent to the introduction of the training levy in the 1970s. Indeed, the impact of the national standards and qualifications movement is already bigger than such innovations as competencies, performance appraisals and assessment centres. We feel that such an important initiative needs to be understood and recognised.

If you suspect we are exaggerating, then remember, that:

- over £70 million of taxpayers' money has been invested by the government in the movement since 1991
- over 1 million NVQs and SVQs have been awarded
- the governments of South Africa, Australia and New Zealand have set up similar systems after reviewing ours
- businesses are claiming massive savings and increases in productivity of employees following competence-based training and development programmes.

The government, NCVQ and SCOTVEC have been the subject of much criticism by those who stand on the sidelines and watch. But there is no doubt that we owe them a great debt for providing Great Britain plc with a powerful tool for human resource development, as well as for the national framework of qualifications. Exactly what that debt is, we will explain.

Sure, there are creases to iron out, many of them concerned with implementation and delivery, but the concept, the approach, and the ideas generated by focusing training and development on competent performance, are powerful. So much so that organisations are adopting the ideas, developing tools and adapting methodologies, even before they are being delivered by the national bodies responsible. We believe that organisations, with their pragmatic approach to what works and what doesn't, together with the government, with its resources and power to influence, are creating a valuable resource for Britain's economy: competent people.

If you thought that the national standards movement was a bureaucracy-ridden waste of time, invented to keep politicians elected and consultants in business, then read on. We will show that national standards and qualifications, developed with taxpayers' money, are a gift horse.

They present the most comprehensive and valuable set of tools ever offered to HR (human resource) professionals.

WHAT'S IN THIS BOOK?

Our book divides into three parts.

- Part One explores why standards and qualifications are important and how they work.
- Part Two shows you how to embed national standards into your organisation, so your people are focusing on improving their performance.
- Part Three shows you how to play with NVQs and SVQs without getting burned.

The separation of Parts Two and Three is an important one, and one which other books have failed to emphasise. You can embed the philosophy of standards into your organisation, and use the tools and methodologies of the national standards and qualifications movement without going near an NVQ or SVQ. In a sense, the qualifications are the icing on the cake. However, their value in accrediting competence and recognising achievement cannot be overstated.

Finally, we have added an Epilogue which evaluates the standards and qualifications movement and the contribution it has made in the past ten years.

HOW CAN I USE THIS BOOK?

You can use this book is several ways:

- If you're simply curious, and you want to find out what it's all about, then skip Parts Two and Three, but read the beginning and end of the book.
- If you need practical advice on improving your HR processes with the use of national standards, but without qualifications, then be sure to read Part Two.
- If you'd like to adopt NVQs and SVQs, then you will need to read the lot.

WHAT STYLE CAN I EXPECT?

Our book is not for the faint-hearted. We tell it like it is, warts and all. If you want a competent workforce and all the financial benefits that brings, it will cost you. What's more, the advice in this book is for those who want to do something well, rather than just play at it. There are few short cuts and no compromise on quality. The style is also very practical. Because we have a substantial amount of experience in a very young field, readers will get a real flavour of what they can expect to happen.

WHO IS THIS BOOK FOR?

Our text is likely to appeal to Human Resource Managers and Training Managers in medium to large enterprises. Those people employed in such organisations who are interested in taking an NVQ/SVQ themselves will also find it of value.

We do not address the concerns of training providers and colleges in delivering NVQs/SVQs. Their needs will be slightly different from those of organisations and their employees. However, as employers themselves, colleges and training providers may find this book of interest in improving the performance of those people who work for them.

We suspect that you are not complete novices. At the very least, you will have heard of NVQs and SVQs and have a vague understanding of how they are different from previous initiatives. You may even have dabbled in embedding the standards or adopting the NVQs/SVQs. Some of you may even be advanced users. Because we discuss the issues and suggest best practice, there is something in this book for both beginners and the cognoscenti.

	Simply curious	HR improver	NVQ/SVQ
Part One	✓	✓	✓
Part Two		✓	✓
Part Three			✓
Epilogue	✓	✓	✓

PART ONE: WHY USE STANDARDS AND NVQs/SVQs?

Let us imagine a personnel or training manager in a British organisation faced with the current challenge to consider NVQs/SVQs. The kinds of questions he or she may be asking are 'What are they?' 'How could they possibly be of any help?' 'Why should I bother when I'm already managing my people development well?'

In this first part of the book, we will argue that human resource management and development can be significantly improved by embedding standards and qualifications into your organisation.

We will show you how:

* the government has seen the value of both standards and qualifications, and has developed the framework within which they sit
* employers too are recognising the benefits of introducing standards and NVQs/SVQs
* a set of national standards can provide you with a description of good practice to which employees should aspire
* the complementary NVQs and SVQs which measure those standards can motivate employees and confirm their competence.

1 WHAT HAS HAPPENED SO FAR?

CHAPTER SUMMARY

We begin by describing why something had to be done to improve the way in which people are trained and assessed in the UK. We outline the crises facing British organisations and describe the importance of people in creating and sustaining success. Finally, we look at the actions taken by both the government and employers, and the progress that has been made since the NVQ/SVQ movement began.

THE NATION'S PERFORMANCE

There is little doubt that when benchmarked against other western economies, Britain is definitely not 'Best in Class'. In 1992, Britain ranked 13th in the World Competitiveness table,[1] behind Ireland and Belgium, countries which have suffered from being the traditional butt of this nation's humour. Although in the last few years we have seen signs of an improvement, it is still a little early to tell if such progress will bring about a real economic turnaround.

In the remainder of this decade, intense challenges from the Pacific Rim economies, and the danger of our own complacency, could force Great Britain plc to slip further downwards in the league tables.

As a response to these unfavourable comparisons, and to economic recession, a competitive culture is emerging in Britain, led by the government and championed by high profile private sector companies, particularly those competing on a world stage, and public sector reformers set on improving the efficiency of the NHS, education and other services and local government.

In May 1994 the government published a White Paper, *Competitiveness: Helping Britain to Win*, laying out what it aimed to achieve in partnership with private enterprise. It stated that the government would provide:
- a stable macroeconomic climate
- efficient market structures
- supportive tax policies
- value for money from public services.

In return, organisations should provide:

- innovation
- good management.

By such measures as deregulation, privatisation and financial support, the government is pursuing its policy of making Britain competitive.

THE IMPORTANCE OF PEOPLE IN A SUCCESSFUL ECONOMY

A number of studies into the amount of money which organisations spend on training and development, have concluded that an investment in training and development is more likely to bring organisational success than not.

However, you should not be beguiled into thinking this a scientific reality. No empirical studies, matching organisation for organisation, have been carried out. Indeed, it is very difficult, if not impossible, to carry them out. That training and development is a key factor in the success of your enterprise has to be believed, rather than conclusively proved. There are so many factors which can result in a successful organisation: the natural energy of the people, inspiring and clear leadership, external conditions, and other factors totally unconnected with the investment in training and development. All of these can make success more likely. However, all of these have one thing in common; they are dependent upon people.

Organisations that ask you to believe their success is due simply to their technological superiority, unique products or ultra-efficient systems are missing the point. While those things are what distinguishes them from others, they are the result of the people who invented, designed, marketed and installed them; then maintained, reviewed and updated them.

It has always been a source of amazement to us that organisations which spend millions of pounds investing in the purchase and maintenance of plant and systems, stint on investing in the very people who will make that investment succeed or fail.

An organisation can invest in recruiting the best people and managing them well. Ultimately, if it wants to keep those people motivated and improving, it has to train and develop them to their highest potential.

By far the most persuasive argument for training people to be competent is the one which rebukes those who claim they cannot afford to train by arguing that, really, they cannot afford *not* to train.

If training and assessment programmes improve performance in an organisation by 0.6 of a standard deviation on the normal performance curve, then this represents a 29% improvement on productivity.[2]

So whether it is empirically proven or not, our instincts tell us that we need to invest in training and development. It cannot be a bad thing.

To return briefly to the assertion that an investment in training and development is more likely to bring organisational success than not, it could well be that those organisations which do invest in training and development are also organisations which appreciate the value of people, and therefore also recruit well, motivate their employees, reward well, and generally sustain higher productivity than those which don't. Again, the direct link between success and investment in training and development is difficult to untangle, but it is probably worth a £10 bet down at Ladbrokes.

This may sound more convincing from the horse's mouth. Steve Gentry, an employee at Upjohn, the pharmaceutical company, explains here the value of training:

> 'Our job at the moment, I wouldn't say it was narrow, but it's only a small part of what goes on. Doing NVQs I've learnt a lot more of what goes on, doing NVQs I've learnt a lot more of what happens outside it; the whole job, more than just my part, what everybody else's job is as well, so many other things I've never realised. We're doing some things and didn't realise why you had to do them, why it had to be like this, and it's only reading through the NVQ units that I found out that if I don't do my part right, then the next person's part won't be right and the problems that follow. Yes it's been very good.'[3]

WHAT THE GOVERNMENT HAS DONE AND WHY

The government's view is that national success depends on our competitiveness and that competitiveness depends, to a large degree, upon the competence, creativity and entrepreneurial flair of its people. An initiative in vocational and professional training is seen as a way of developing such qualities.

Good organisations don't have to be told these things by government. They will do it anyway. But some organisations have not trained and developed their people well. Why is this? Is it a lack of will or a lack of way? Or both?

Well, the government's response has been to provide carrots rather than sticks. The stick would have been the introduction of a statutory obligation to train and develop staff. But the current Conservative government and the Labour opposition have both said that they hope to avoid such a tax. Instead, the government is offering two things: tax incentives to train and develop people within the NVQ/SVQ framework, and tools, techniques and processes to help organisations provide better training and development.

What the government has done is to:

- ask industry and commerce to set out its own standards for each occupation in Britain
- ensure that those standards are in the public domain and organisations are encouraged to use them
- concentrate on demonstrated competence in the workplace rather than learning in the classroom
- rationalise the entire structure of vocational qualifications so that it is simple and consistent
- set out a number of national training targets which need to be achieved by the end of the century
- develop a number of initiatives and incentives such as Investors in People, National Training Awards, setting up of TECs and LECs which are designed to improve training and development in Britain.

HOW ORGANISATIONS HAVE REACTED AND WHY

The NVQ/SVQ movement began formally in 1986 with the establishment of the National Council for Vocational Qualifications. Initially, the response from organisations was muted because it didn't affect them to a large extent. However, those organisations that were approached to help in the first developments were very positive, especially the trade unions. It took the first couple of years to develop all the machinery, design the system and make available the first sets of standards and qualifications. Gradually, as more and more standards and qualifications are put in place, more and more organisations are looking at them and deciding if they wish to take part.

The surprise response has been how quickly organisations have accepted the notion of standards and begun embedding them into their HR systems, irrespective of whether or not the organisations are embracing the NVQs/SVQs. The government has set national training targets for the numbers of people following and completing NVQs/SVQs.

National training targets

- By 1997, 80% of young people to reach NVQ 2 or equivalent
- By 1997, 63% of young people to achieve either five GCSEs at

grades A–C, an NVQ 2 or equivalent
- By 2000, 50% of young people to reach NVQ 3 or equivalent
- By 2000, 41% of young people to achieve either two A levels, an NVQ 3 or equivalent
- By 2000, 50% of the workforce qualified to two A levels, NVQ level 3 or equivalent or a higher qualification.[4]

The government should also be pleased that standards are being used to improve the competence of the British workforce. Perhaps the government should consider recording the extent to which standards are being embedded into organisations, as well as the number of NVQs/SVQs awarded.

WHAT ARE NATIONAL STANDARDS AND HOW DO THEY WORK?

They are standards of competence, and apply to people rather than to products. The standards are simply descriptions of what needs to be achieved in a work activity. However, they are written in a very particular way. Rather than describing the way things need to be done, they describe the outcomes of those activities. They always include:

- the element of competence which describes the activity
- a description of the criteria by which success in that activity will be judged
- the range of circumstances in which those activities should be carried out
- the knowledge and understanding which underpins the activity
- the types of evidence one would need in order to confirm that someone is competent

and occasionally,

- the personal competencies or qualities which would help someone achieve the standard.

Standards are derived in a very particular way using interested parties: groups of employers and employees in the relevant occupation, training providers, educators. Mr Bloggs, who owns the travel agency in the high street, could not go ahead and write the national standards for travel agents. But he may be invited to join a number of other travel agents, from different backgrounds, under the auspices of the lead body for the travel sector, sometimes with the help of a consultant, to write the national standards.

Together they will use a technique called functional analysis in order to capture a comprehensive picture of the whole activity. This provides a very clear description of:

- the technical skills that are required
- the ability to manage contingencies and unexpected problems
- the organisational skills to complete this activity and others to achieve an overall objective
- the ability to get on with others and cope with the natural conditions and constraints in the workplace.

So the national standards:

- focus on what people can do as well as what they know
- are laid out in a way that makes expectations very clear
- look at all aspects of performance, not just technical skills
- provide a statement of good practice, endorsed at a national level.

WHAT ARE NVQs/SVQs AND HOW DO THEY WORK?

NVQs/SVQs are qualifications awarded to those who can demonstrate that they have achieved the national standards. They make a break from traditional examination practices. Instead of assessing candidates through examinations, the focus of assessment has shifted to the workplace, where employees assess other employees carrying out their normal jobs against national standards. Sometimes a visiting assessor carries out this role, but more usually it is another member of staff. NVQs and SVQs therefore demand more imaginative, new and more varied forms of assessment.

Because it is competence we are judging here, not learning, the assessment relies heavily on different types of evidence:

- things people have done
- products people have made
- records they have kept
- reports they have written
- things other people have said about their work.

In short, the assessment is based on a wide range of evidence. The process of assessment is continuous, until enough evidence has been seen to judge the candidate competent or otherwise. Previous accomplishments can be taken into account, and the candidate can get the qualification without taking any specified programme of learning.

The practical benefits of this approach are obvious:

- intimate involvement in the process by both of the main stakeholders: employers and employees
- flexible assessment programmes which
  - are tailored to each individual
  - are followed at the individual's own pace
- accessible qualifications which
  - have no barriers to age, gender, time served or experience
  - are appropriate to both trainees and more experienced staff
  - are not tied into a timetable of examinations, or assessment cycle.

There have been objections to this new approach, however. The most widely publicised is described below.

THE SMITHERS DEBATE

In December 1993 Professor Alan Smithers of Manchester University assisted Channel Four in the preparation of a 'Dispatches' documentary programme about the standards and NVQ/SVQ movement.[5] His principal criticism of the movement was that in concentrating on competence, the importance of knowledge and understanding was being ignored. He concluded that people qualified by the NVQ route might be capable of performing in the workplace but they may not understand what they were doing. He supported his arguments with comparisons with vocational training in Germany, where a broader knowledge base is provided during training.

NCVQ's response was clear, although more muted than one would have hoped. It rested on two rebuttals: that the programme had been biased; and that the assertions made in it were false. In both cases we believe they were right, although complaining to the media for lack of fairness is like complaining to the government for being too party political.

NCVQ believes that the assertion made by Professor Smithers that NVQs disregard the requirement for knowledge overlooks the facts. First of all, NCVQ's own published criteria explicitly state that NVQs require the separate assessment of knowledge where this is necessary to infer competence. Secondly, NCVQ points out that 'written questions and answers' are indeed mentioned in their literature as a suitable means of assessment.

NCVQ defended the importance of knowledge and understanding within their NVQs with ample evidence from their publications, and examples of qualifications showing how it can be separately identified and assessed. And, although NCVQ did illustrate their point by stating that written examinations are included in NVQs in Accounting and Pensions Administration, even they would admit that that's a tiny proportion of the qualifications they have accredited.

There is no doubt that the Smithers controversy touched a raw nerve within the standards movement and that the importance of knowledge and understanding will be made more explicit from now on in the design of training and assessment for NVQs. But some temporary damage has been done to the credibility of the movement simply because of the ill-informed way in which the debate was presented to the public.

TRAINING AND QUALIFICATIONS AT HOME AND ABROAD

It is always a good idea, though, to look at other developed countries and compare their systems with ours. Comparisons are often made between France, Germany and the UK. *Towards a Skills Revolution*, the report of the Vocational Education and Training Task Force, showed that the percentage of the workforce holding university entrance level qualifications was:

- France 35%
- Germany 30%
- Britain 15%.

Indeed, France has targeted to have 60% of its people in higher education by the turn of the century.

But it is also important to point out that the vocational training and qualification system that has been put in place in Britain is creating great interest from around the world. To date, there have been visits and enquiries to NCVQ from 39 countries worldwide and identical or similar systems are being developed abroad with the help of NCVQ and the British Council.

VOCATIONAL AND ACADEMIC ROUTES

In France and Germany, the focus has been on higher and further education rather than on training; and on academic rather than vocational qualifications, hence the figures above. Perhaps an important issue to be tackled in this country is the creation of a similar world-beating framework for academic qualifications. General National Vocational Qualifications (GNVQs), it has to be said, have made a start here. GNVQs are designed to provide the skills and vocationally oriented knowledge for progression to NVQs/SVQs and further learning, including entrance into higher education.

NVQs/SVQs and GNVQs then, although aiming at different markets and outcomes, both appear to be contributing to an increased appreciation of the value of education and training.

'It was stimulating and it's prompted me to go on and do a part-time university course, which I am now half way through, so it was a direct result of that and because of my results in the NVQ I was accepted as a university student; they took that as proof of educational standards.'[6]

RECOMMENDATIONS

Much has been achieved in the ten or so years since the standards movement began. There is still a long way to go to ensure that this initiative is contributing fully to improving the efficiency and effectiveness of organisations. But the general feeling amongst the practitioners we know is that we are going in the right direction and, coupled with a willingness to review and improve constantly, much can be achieved. It would be worthwhile to:

* watch closely for Britain's movement in the world economic tables over the next few years
* remember the critical role played by competent people in the success of an organisation and be prepared to invest in them.

NOTES

1 *World Competitiveness Report* compiled by World Economic Forum and International Institute for Management (IMD), Lausanne. Reported in *CBI News*, November 1994.
2 M Burke and R Day 'A Cumulative Study of the Effectiveness of Managerial Training', *Journal of Applied Psychology* (April–June 1986).
3 *Going for NVQs* audio cassette and workbook, produced by the Chemical Industries Association.
4 Report on Progress Towards the National Targets (NACETT, July 1995).
5 *All Our Futures: Britain's Education Revolution* (Channel Four 'Dispatches', 15 December 1993).
6 *Going for NVQs* audio cassette and workbook, produced by the Chemical Industries Association.

2 HOW CAN NATIONAL STANDARDS HELP IMPROVE PERFORMANCE?

CHAPTER SUMMARY

Managing people is difficult, we need all the help we can get. We err into subjective and conflicting judgements about people all too easily. Standards offer a simple structure to help managers concentrate on performance, and in so doing, help them to encourage the performance that is required and make objective assessments about people's competence. This chapter describes the plethora of different ways in which we specify what we want from people, points out the confusion that exists and suggests that using national standards as a focus for these HR activities will provide both increased objectivity and a more coherent structure.

THE ROLE OF STANDARDS

Everyone at work needs to know what they are required to do; so that they can agree with it, disagree with it, do it, not do it, change it, measure themselves against it or simply disregard it. But without the clear specification of acceptable performance, very few human resource (HR) processes can take place. For example, training and development activities need clear objectives. Appraisal processes need criteria for evaluation. Managers need clear requirements to manage performance.

Without standards, two problems permeate human resource management (HRM) and human resource development (HRD) processes and most of the approaches which underpin them. There are large elements of *subjectivity* in reaching decisions about performance, and there is a *lack of coherence* between different HR processes.

TOO MUCH SUBJECTIVITY

Subjectivity can creep in at every stage in the management and development of people, but particularly in recruitment, in appraisal, and in reward. Let's face it, people are the most complex thing that any of us ever encounter. When assessing others, we need as much help as possible.

To be fair to the individual, and to make best use of talent for the organisation, we need to overcome our own biases, cowardice and lack of understanding. If we are to make good decisions about who should be given a role, how to encourage them to give their best, and how to measure how well they are doing and particularly what they should be paid, then it is incumbent upon us all to strive for objectivity. National standards can help provide that objectivity.

The process of describing clearly the criteria by which to judge people at work is a very tricky one. It is intellectually demanding and requires persistence. Newcomers to our field take several weeks before they acquire the knack of learning to write objective statements of performance. Understanding the kind of thing that's required is not difficult, but finding the right words to express it is.

It is all too easy, as we know, to end up having made the measurable things important, instead of the important things measurable. Struggling with the vagaries of the English language only adds to the difficulty. Managers may simply not have the skills to describe performance requirements objectively or comprehensively. Perhaps this is why some HR processes, such as appraisal, are still resisted; because those subjected to them have little faith in the criteria being applied.

When it comes to the assessment process itself, many managers find objective assessment difficult. Talking at an intimate level with another person about their performance requires considerable skill and maturity. They may end up assessing what the person intended to do, rather than what was actually done. They may end up considering evidence which is spurious or hearsay, when they intended only to consider what was valid and reliable. Worst of all, they may end up ignoring the criteria and assessing someone on a negative gut feeling about him or her. Particularly worrying is the situation where people are rewarded on the strength of their having 'blue eyes'. We've all done one or other of these, I'm sure. But we might have been less subjective if we had had clear, objective, agreed performance requirements, such as those provided by national standards.

TOO LITTLE COHERENCE

All HR processes need to be coordinated if they are to work together to produce the kind of people which the organisation needs. If they don't, if they are based on different approaches, principals or criteria, then people will get very confused.

For example, the purpose of someone's employment, as specified in a job description or role definition should not be different to the measures used in their appraisal; the aims and objectives of their training and development should be aligned to the factors on which their performance is measured; their reward should be based on something similar to their understanding of what they are there for.

Typically, HR processes are described in different and often confusing language. We have a plethora of different ways of describing what is required of people in the workplace. To ease the confusion, we suggest that standards provide a coherent focus for developing all HR processes.

Imagine the typical processes that people go through in employment: people are recruited, inducted, trained and developed, their performance is managed on an ongoing basis, they are rewarded and, when appropriate, they are released or redeployed. Let's take each step in this cycle in turn.

We enter into this cycle of activities on a day-to-day basis using a variety of tools and processes. However, if we look more closely at how we describe our performance expectations for each stage in the cycle, we may realise that we do it differently each time.

Figure 2.1 HR processes

Recruitment

The specifications we use for recruitment include person specifications, job descriptions, interview criteria and assessment centre criteria.

Sometimes job advertisements also contain useful information not specified elsewhere. However, they do not usually contain a set of standards that recruits to the organisation should either have already met or which they will be required to meet. The result is that people are often recruited into organisations unclear of the exact nature of their role, and unaware of the standards that are being applied to them.

Training and development

The specifications for training and development usually include aims, goals, objectives, lists of content, scope of materials and syllabuses of learning, but not standards.

The result is that training can end up meeting its own self-fulfilling objectives, but overlooking the application of that learning on the job, or the outcomes of successful performance.

Performance management

To manage performance effectively, people use job descriptions, and appraisal criteria such as competencies, behaviours, skills, key result areas, targets, and codes of conduct (often implicit and unwritten).

Much of performance management is about helping individuals, in their day-to-day role, to maintain good standards of professional or occupational practice. Without performance standards, that's not going to happen!

Reward

Performance is usually rewarded by assessment against specifications such as targets and agreed objectives but, again, not standards.

The result is that individuals are encouraged and motivated to work towards specific, quantitative, annual targets, ignoring general good practice.

Release and redeployment

In making decisions about releasing or redeploying people, one might consider what has been done, what results have been achieved and what next career steps could be taken.

Standards have a useful role to play here in specifying requirements quite precisely.

Even more useful, though, is where release or redeployment is not voluntary, such as in dismissal. Then the criteria used have to be very focused and objective. Usually codes of practice, poor performance and appraisal results, and failure to meet targets are used to identify such individuals. But again, standards would help in clarifying the reasons for dismissal.

Specifying requirements

Let's look at a typical job description.

JOB DESCRIPTION		
Job title	Grade	
Department	Reports to	
Main functions of job		
Liability for cash/stock deficiencies		
Location		
Supervisory responsibilities		
Main duties: Duties/responsibilities	% time to be spent	Level of responsibility

Tools and equipment used
Working conditions/degree of effort required
Qualifications/education required
Experience required
Specialist training required
Any particular aptitude/skill required

Figure 2.2 Typical items included in a job description

This example lists what should be done, but gives no indication of how well those things should be done, or how anyone would know when they have been done correctly.

The effect of this is to leave people to work out their own understanding of requirements, which may or may not be the same as their colleagues' and managers'.

USING STANDARDS TO DEFINE PERFORMANCE REQUIREMENTS

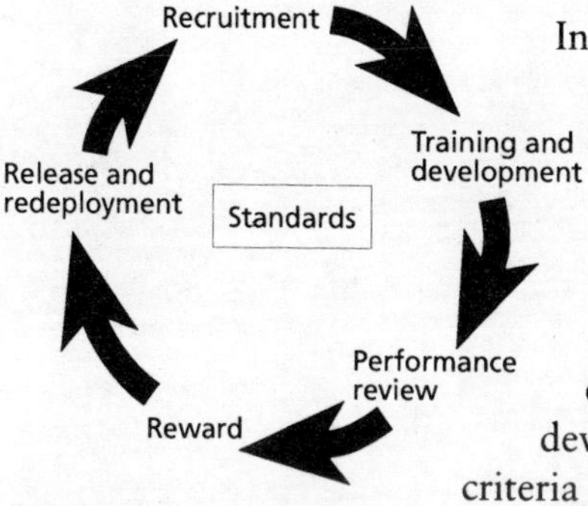

Figure 2.3 HR processes built around standards

In a standards culture, all the different processes for managing and developing human resources are built around the same set of standards for the role.

The standards give rise to criteria for selection and recruitment. They drive the induction, training and development of a person. They are the criteria on which performance is managed (including appraisal). And they provide the measures against which people are rewarded, released and redeployed.

For example, the job description for an HR manager might list, amongst other things, the maintenance of a suitable HR strategy. Adding a set of standards to the job description enables the HR manager to know how his or her performance in that area will be judged.

JOB: HR Manager

DUTIES INCLUDE: Developing the HR strategy

STANDARDS:

- *A strategy is in place which has been updated in the last six months (or sooner)*
- *It is in written form and has been disseminated to all those who need to know*
- *It provides the necessary people initiatives to support the business strategy.*

Figure 2.4 Some duties and standards for an HR manager

Another example, taken from a set of standards we have prepared for those who handle the telephone in organisations, shows how company standards can be incorporated.

JOB: Supervisor

DUTIES INCLUDE: Handling incoming calls

STANDARDS:

- *Calls are answered within three double-rings*
- *Calls are diverted to appropriate person*
- *Friendly greeting ('Good morning/afternoon') and identification is given*
- *Calls requiring routine responses are actioned promptly*
- *Companies soliciting business are politely but firmly declined unless of particular interest*
- *Messages taken for others show*
  - *time and date of call*
  - *who message is for*
  - *priority*
  - *subject of message*
  - *action required*
  - *contact name, number and organisation of caller*

Figure 2.5 Some duties and standards for a supervisor

Yet another example, this time using national standards, lists quite clearly the good practice that is expected of anyone providing counselling or advice to members of the public.

JOB: Adviser

DUTIES INCLUDE: Providing advice to clients

STANDARDS: Agree ways of working with clients

- *Clients' expectations and understanding of the service and its policy are clarified with them*
- *Roles in achieving the required outcomes from the service are discussed and agreed*
- *Ways in which clients can give feedback and evaluate the service are discussed and agreed with them*
- *Clients' preferred ways of working are taken into account in making a clear agreement with them about using the service*
- *Completed records are accurate, stored in a suitable manner and conform to policy on confidentiality*

Figure 2.6 Some duties and standards for an adviser

Standards, either national standards which you can import into your HR processes, or those you have written yourself, bring you a description of good performance which can offer the objectivity and coherence that you require for your HR processes.

We are not suggesting that standards replace all the other ways we have of describing performance in the workplace. A set of national standards could never be expected to do the job of, for example, a site code of conduct, or a company-specific procedure. Nor could national standards, which describe good practice in a whole occupation, specify individual targets.

But the ways in which national standards are written provide you with a fund of useful information. Importing an existing set of national standards will save you having to do the work yourself and possibly falling into some of the traps we mentioned earlier because:

- they have been prepared by people who represent the highest standards in a profession or occupation, and who know how to write standards
- they have been endorsed nationally
- they include all the important aspects of a job
- they are available for all (or nearly all) occupations in Britain.

RECOMMENDATIONS

We suggest that you:

- look at the sample standards above and in Appendix 1 and decide for yourself whether or not they add value to the way you currently prescribe performance
- consider how much more objective and consistent your HR practices would be if you had a set of standards against which to manage performance.

The next chapter takes you through the implications of adopting a standards culture and helps you to decide if that route is for you.

3 WHY GET INVOLVED?

CHAPTER SUMMARY

By now you may be toying with the idea of using standards to update your job descriptions and appraisal systems or you may even be contemplating the idea of implementing an NVQ or SVQ.

But whatever you are planning, you should be aware of what will happen if you take this road. We will take you through the consequences of getting involved, so that you are in a position to decide if the benefits are worth the costs. We will outline the areas of major change, highlight areas that will concern people, raise questions over the timing of introducing standards and offer guidance on the costs.

THE BENEFITS OF USING STANDARDS

Many people working in this field have claimed that using national standards brings benefits, for example:

> *'At Boots we like to think that we have always provided good quality training and development programmes for all our staff. We have always seen this training as being essential if we are to achieve our business plans and if we are to deliver that quality of service we have always demanded from our people.*
>
> *When reviewing our training provision for sales assistants about three years ago, we saw the potential of supplementing our programme with an incentive for staff to achieve recognised qualifications.*
>
> *We were delighted with the results which showed improved standards of recruitment, raised standards of performance, improved quality of training, better motivated staff and increased retention of staff.'*
>
> *Gordon Hourston, Managing Director, Boots the Chemist*

Similarly, claims are made for increased flexibility, motivation and improved morale.

> *'NVQs are providing working people with tremendous opportunities to increase their skills and their contribution to better business performance and to gain national recognised qualifications in the process.'*
>
> *John Adshead, Personnel Director, J Sainsbury plc*

But many of these benefits are ones which should result if good training and qualifications are put in place in an organisation anyway. They are not exclusively the result of the national standards and qualifications movement.

ACHIEVING OBJECTIVITY

The benefits of using standards come from objectively defining and measuring performance. The benefits of adopting standards are a competent workforce. But because of the objectivity that comes with standards, be prepared for a culture shock. People will be far clearer about what they are required to do. Consequently, they will want a bigger say in decisions about their performance and how their work is organised and managed.

Therefore, before reaching a decision on whether to use standards as a focus for HRM or to go as far as to introduce an NVQ or SVQ, it is only fair to warn you about what you are letting yourself in for and identify areas that will need to be carefully managed.

Armed with this information you will be able to reach an informed decision about whether your organisation will be able to cope with and manage the changes that the introduction of standards will bring. However, do not let this put you off. The introduction of HR processes that improve business performance deserves an investment of time and energy to make sure that they are developed and managed effectively.

MANAGING CHANGE

What follows is a list of the areas that will need to be carefully managed, because they may cause various people concern.

Standards will expose gaps

Through the use of standards, gaps in people's knowledge and skills will be exposed, but they will also recognise strengths. However, some may feel threatened because they may not feel comfortable at having their weaknesses highlighted. They will feel less vulnerable if they know that the gaps are being exposed to help them. People should be reassured that additional skills will help them perform better in their jobs and perhaps make them more secure.

Therefore, be prepared to organise structured training packages. The use of standards may even result in deciding that a person is in the wrong job. Perhaps a person's skills would be better employed doing something else. Be prepared to recognise strengths and even identify people for promotion.

Standards may be a burden

Employees may think that the methods you devise to review their performance are a burden. They may already be busy and under pressure and find it difficult to integrate the review procedures into their normal routines and working patterns.

Therefore, introduce simple systems and processes based on what already happens in the workplace.

Experienced employees may object

If employees have been doing jobs for some time, are experienced and may even hold a handful of formal qualifications, they may feel that their professional integrity is being called into question. They may believe that you are trying to catch them out and that if they do not meet the standards, then they might be identified as candidates for redundancy or early retirement.

Therefore, be prepared to assure people that standards are being used to manage their performance and that there will be opportunities to assess areas not normally covered by traditional examinations. Explain that standards can also be used to identify opportunities for progression, career development, promotion or redeployment into other areas of the business. In our experience we have discovered that people like to know the requirements of the job and develop the skills required, if only they are given the opportunity.

People will want a greater say in decisions over their performance

Employees will be able to complete their work more effectively by having standards against which to benchmark performance. They will be better informed and focused and therefore able to make suggestions on how to do their jobs more efficiently.

Therefore, be prepared to listen to suggestions from employees on how working practices can be changed, updated and improved.

Employees may expect too much

Employees' expectations may be raised too high. As employees become more competent they will want to take a more active role, but they will need to understand the limitations of their new freedoms. With freedom comes responsibility. Employees will need to understand that final decisions are still the responsibility of their managers, otherwise employees will become frustrated and demotivated.

Therefore, be prepared to help them come to terms with what is expected of them. They will need systems or frameworks in which they can work. They will need to know how to make suggestions and discuss ideas with their managers.

Managers may be suspicious

As people learn more about their jobs and their contribution to the business, they will have ideas on how to do their jobs more effectively. They may ask for more responsibility and see opportunities to develop their jobs. Some managers may not be comfortable with this.

Therefore, be prepared to help some managers change their role to one of developing staff and managing ideas. They will need to know how to accept or reject ideas, without killing off any enthusiasm.

Line managers may feel threatened

As employees become more competent they will probably need less supervision. As their skills and knowledge improve, it may not be necessary to check their work as often as before. Line managers who have traditionally checked up on people may have to change their role.

Therefore, be prepared to help line managers develop their roles, where they will be required to manage staff by setting objectives, leading teams and identifying training needs.

A CHANGING ROLE FOR PERSONNEL AND TRAINING FUNCTIONS

Because employees are assessed in the workplace, line managers will need to assume responsibility. This means that human resource departments will lose some of their traditional functions.

Therefore, be prepared to change the role of training and personnel departments, because they will now be responsible for providing the advice, stimulus and know-how. A bit like the charity Oxfam, their role will be to provide other departments with the tools and expertise so they can manage improvement in performance themselves.

Standards will change training arrangements

The amount of money organisations spend training people can be difficult to calculate nationally because decisions are often made locally. However, employers have not always spent money evaluating whether the training met the needs of the employees and business. However, if people have a set of standards to benchmark themselves against, they will be able to judge whether a particular training programme provided them with the skills and knowledge to carry out their duties.

Therefore, be prepared for employees to criticise training programmes. The investment of time updating training programmes will be well worth the effort, because it is likely that you will hear the following complaint less frequently: 'I had a nice time, but it didn't help me.'

Time may not be available

The processes you develop to appraise performance will have to be administered, managed and carried out. Employees may already be busy. Managers may see them as instrusive.

Therefore, be prepared to help managers and their employees understand that managing performance on the basis of standards is an investment. The processes you develop should help managers review performance, set objectives and identify training needs. Be ready with a list of the benefits to present to them. If necessary, be prepared to remind them gently that this is something they should be doing anyway.

Local help may not be forthcoming

You may discover that you will need outside help. You may identify a training need, in which case you may seek help from a local college or training provider. However, local trainers may only be able to offer you off-the-shelf courses. They may not be willing to tailor or develop programmes to meet your requirements.

Therefore, be prepared to work in partnership with local training providers. You will have to explain that they should be far more customer driven by responding to your needs. A number of local colleges are responding in this way but, if they are to remain in business, much still needs to be done.

Consequences

So standards can change the culture of your organisation. People will want a bigger say in decisions about their performance. People will understand more about what they are required to do, the business needs and how their efforts contribute to the success or failure of the organisation.

In an organisation that is not using standards, employees can have an easier life. They can blame under-achievement and the failure of a project on the absence of clarity and a clear description of what is expected. They can blame poor results on insufficient sets of written procedures and the absence of clear instructions. How often do we hear the complaint: 'It's not my fault, I didn't know that he wanted me to do that'?

An organisation that uses standards or NVQs/SVQs leaves little to chance. High levels of performance are required and appraised. However, standards do not tie people down. By enjoying more clarity, employees are more likely to be creative and innovative. Judgements about a person's performance will have to be objective, thereby removing the temptation towards subjectivity.

YOUR ORGANISATION'S CULTURE

Bearing in mind that the introduction of standards may be threatening and may cause a culture shock, make sure your organisation is ready by considering the health of your organisation and deciding whether it is sufficiently robust to respond to the demands. We know of a family-run business that can be described as feudal, where a father and two sons make all the decisions. For those of you old enough to remember, it can be likened to the department store called Grace Brothers in the TV series 'Are You Being Served?'. Out of deference, employees even refer to the sons as Mr John and Mr Ian.

It would be fair to say that employees are strait-jacketed. Although this company invited us to talk to them about using national standards we have discouraged them. They have now recognised that they have a long way to go in changing the culture. We have advised them to start with a few small projects and gradually introduce the notion of involving staff in how their jobs are organised, appraised and reviewed.

In assessing your own circumstances and deciding whether your company is in a position to use standards or introduce an NVQ or SVQ, it might be useful to compare your organisation with the following scenarios.

- *Sink or swim*. Perhaps your organisation is in the unfortunate position of facing a threat to its survival, and there is pressure to make massive changes because of serious competition from rivals. If you want to compete successfully, developing a competent, innovative and flexible human resource can be an essential ingredient of your rescue package.

- *Not another flavour of the month.* Is your organisation suffering from initiative overload? If you have introduced a complex initiative recently, employees may need a period of stability so that they can feel more settled and confident about the future.
- *Not receptive to new ideas.* What is the culture of your organisation like? If your management system is rigid and inflexible, you may need a period of more gradual change in order to introduce employees slowly to the changes that will take place.
- *Fat cats.* Is your organisation growing stale? Perhaps there is a feeling of contentment and living off the fat of the land. If you want to stimulate enthusiasm and avoid inevitable decline, the introduction of standards may do the trick.
- *Making changes.* Perhaps your organisation has a major change programme, such as Total Quality or Investors in People. If you want to review whether this change has been both appropriate and effective, then the introduction of standards or NVQs/SVQs may provide you with the measure you need.

HOW FAR TO GO

So, having given you the information about what to expect, having warned you about the changes that will take place and asked you to consider the health of your organisation, you should now be in a position to decide whether to use standards or go the whole hog and introduce an NVQ or SVQ. You are of course best placed to decide whether the investment is worth the effort.

Whatever route you take, from our experience we would advise you to start small. If you use standards to develop your HR processes, then pick one area to develop your system. For example, use standards as a focus for developing or updating an appraisal system. If you want to introduce an NVQ or SVQ, run a small pilot first with one occupational group made up of a small group of volunteers.

By keeping your activities small, you will be able to control what is happening. Do not run the risk of failing on a big scale. It can be difficult to reinstate the use of standards or an NVQ/SVQ if it falls at the first hurdle.

COST CONSIDERATIONS

Your organisation is probably already training staff, conducting appraisals and reviewing progress. A lot of the costs identified below are probably already being spent. Therefore, it is unlikely that huge amounts of additional indirect or direct costs will be incurred to introduce standards or an NVQ/SVQ.

Indirect costs

Indirect costs will be incurred by a centre mainly in relation to how much time is spent developing, implementing and reviewing your systems for human resource development. You will need time to:

- identify which sets of national standards are available for the different occupations carried out in your organisation
- become familiar with relevant standards
- update or develop your systems for human resource development, which could include rewriting job descriptions, appraisal systems, training programmes and the criteria for rewarding employees
- implement the systems you have developed; such as briefing staff, organising meetings and running training sessions
- enlist the help of colleagues from other departments
- engage the support of senior managers
- oversee the use of the systems
- review and evaluate what has happened as a result
- update the systems based on practical experience and feedback.

Direct costs

Money may be spent on the direct costs of:

- printing documents such as guide notes, briefing papers, training materials, policy statements, job descriptions and appraisal forms
- sending people on training courses
- purchasing open learning materials and training courses
- paying college and examination fees
- registering with an awarding body if you decide to offer NVQs or SVQs, where you will probably be charged for:
  - the relevant publications
  - seeking centre approval

- training and assessing those staff who are running the assessment process
- registering candidates with the awarding body
- requesting unit certificates or NVQs/SVQs from the awarding body
- additional visits by the awarding body's external verifier
- attending conferences seminars and workshops.

We believe that the initial development and start-up costs associated with using standards as a focus for developing your human resource areas are well worth the effort. Organisations using standards claim that they actually save money.

BENEFITS CASE STUDY

Rather than take our word for it, here are the facts from a user who made substantial savings by introducing NVQs/SVQs into a part of his organisation.

In the engineering department at ICI Chemicals and Polymers Merseyside Operations we have measured how NVQs have benefited the business. This is why we use them.

ICI C&P have achieved many of the benefits that we were seeking. From 1990 to 1993:

- *Fixed expense of maintaining production plants has dropped by 20% per unit*
- *There have been significant reductions in the manpower required for specific tasks – the improvement on some overhauls has been as much as 50%*
- *Absenteeism and sickness have halved*
- *All injury frequency has halved*

The quality of the operations has also been significantly improved:

- *There has been a measurable simplification in planning tasks through the ability to use teams with mixed skills rather than individuals with demarcated skills*
- *Improvement in problem solving skills has led to fewer plant breakdowns with consequent savings of financial and other resources*
- *Workmanship and quality of work has improved significantly. For instance, on one plant, the number of remade joints leaking on start-up has dropped from 35% four years ago to less than 5% now*
- *Highly qualified engineers are freed up to solve advanced technical problems*
- *The number of people involved in improvements has more than trebled in three years*
- *The speed of culture change within the organisation has been increased by the injection of the new students and their mentors into the operations*

There is concrete evidence of culture change as a result of the staff development:

- *Increased competence of staff has led to the removal of a complete layer of management and the need for less supervisors*

- *Employees are proactive in suggesting improvements, and they report solutions rather than problems*
- *Shop floor people have been trained as trainers and assessors, thereby enhancing their skills and competence*

In addition top management can be confident that:

- *individuals are capable of safely, properly and completely fulfilling their tasks*
- *newly graduated trainees are really ready to add value to the company*
- *a steady stream of people committed to the new culture is being injected into the company both as new recruits and at the crucial level of first line management*
- *an increasing proportion of the management structure, currently 18%, have now gained their positions through rigorous recognition of competence and skills.*
- *overall, employees are more motivated and are finding their jobs more satisfying.*

QUOTES

'We are getting the £3–400,000 a year that we spend on these programmes back several times over.'

'With NVQs you have to plan and be meticulous. It is all about competence as observed by a qualified assessor.'

'If you are considering using NVQs, there are some important steps that you should take:

- *Look carefully at your own needs before approaching an awarding body*
- *Plan carefully and think what you want to get out of an NVQ/SVQ*
- *Target a business area, start small and spread later*
- *Pilot the scheme. Show success and then advertise it to develop interest*
- *Peer pressure is significant in building employee interest*
- *Feed people with individual units at first. An NVQ/SVQ could be frightening.'*

Peter Hyam, Engineering Manager

RECOMMENDATIONS

Introducing and using standards to assess competence will bring many beneficial changes. But this chapter was designed to help you identify what you will need to consider before going ahead and what areas you will need to manage if you do.

You should remember that:

- you may meet resistance from staff because a standards-based approach will be unfamiliar and threatening
- people at all levels may feel vulnerable
- initial development and start-up costs will be incurred
- the tools developed to manage performance are used in the workplace by members of your own workforce

- all staff will need to understand the benefits and what needs to be done
- your organisation has its own culture and that the timing of the introduction of standards may be important
- job roles will change
- people are your most valuable resource, all their talents will be needed to make the standards work
- organisations are already benefiting and may be stealing a lead.

PART TWO: EMBEDDING STANDARDS

If you have read Part One, you will have formed your own view of the benefits and implications of embracing the standards movement. To add more detail, this part of the book provides practical advice on how to embed standards into your HR processes.

Remember, you can use national standards in your organisation fruitfully without ever touching an NVQ or SVQ. If, however, you want to go the full distance and adopt qualifications as well, then you should read Part Three as well as Part Two.

4 PRACTICAL ADVICE ON EMBEDDING STANDARDS

CHAPTER SUMMARY

This chapter begins by looking at exactly what a standards culture is and asks you whether or not you have a standards culture in your organisation. It describes types of standards which you may use in your organisation and shows how using national standards will add to the measuring and monitoring of performance that you already undertake. It then describes in detail the uses to which standards can be put in recruiting, developing, managing, rewarding, releasing and redeploying people.

WHAT KINDS OF ORGANISATIONS HAVE A STANDARDS CULTURE?

Many organisations are used to thinking about standards, however they are defined. The engineering and processing industries, for example, have readily embraced the standards culture because standards are, for them, a way of life.

For example, health and safety standards are a constant concern in many sectors. Visiting sites all over the country we are frequently reminded of the priority given to safety by billboards near the site entrance which publicise the site's accident record for the preceding month. Environmental standards in sectors such as chemicals, waste and electricity generation take the standards which apply to them very seriously, publishing regular figures on whether or not they are achieving the standards set out for them.

In the manufacturing sector, organisations are also familiar with and work to standards. British Standards for products are probably the oldest and most familiar to many of us. But additionally, some industries such as the food and drink industry and pharmaceutical manufacturing are used to frequent inspections from various regulatory bodies; for example, the Food and Drinks Inspectorate, Food and Drugs Administration.

There are other, far more contentious examples too: the education service, for instance, is publishing information on school performance and their results are being sorted into league tables. Until recently, the league tables have been fairly crude, presenting data on examination performance only. But other measures are being added, such as amount of time spent on curricular and extra-curricular activities and attendance rates.

The NHS Trusts have responded to criticisms of their crude statistics by publishing more sophisticated information than mere death rates in their hospitals. They have added measures such as:

- the number of days after a hip replacement in which the patient is discharged from the hospital trust
- the amount of health education provided to the community
- the number of teenage pregnancies in the catchment area
- the coverage of their vaccination programmes.

Both British Rail and London Underground have performance standards for the efficiency of their networks and their performance is published monthly at railway and underground stations, as part of the Passenger Charter Initiative.

So all in all, there is an increase in the requirement to publish performance data and to use them for comparative purposes.

Most of the examples cited so far illustrate the case where standards are applied by government or other statutory authorities on organisations. But increasingly, we are finding a fascination with measurement of performance from within the organisation, and a will to set its own targets and publicise its own achievement.

ASSESSING YOUR CURRENT EXPERIENCE

Any experience using standards of any kind will be helpful to organisations because their culture may already include an appreciation of measurement. But organisations which have never assessed themselves against standards may find the adoption of our approach difficult or unfamiliar.

For example, both the police force and the medical profession have resisted individual performance appraisal. And organisations in which there is a high concentration of entrepreneurial or self-managed people, such as in a barrister's chambers, are likely to resist any tool which makes them accountable.

It is worth considering for a moment where your organisation is in this picture.

- Do you lay out your organisational goals in detail? For the whole organisation? For individual functions or departments?
- Do you measure the performance of your organisation against your own organisational goals?
- Do you benchmark your performance against other organisations?

- Do you adopt national benchmarks for your organisation, such as ISO9000 and IIP?
- Do you measure individual performance against the individual's own goals?
- Do you measure individual performance against national standards?

If you were able to answer 'yes' to most of these, then you are already in the kind of culture which could readily embrace national standards. If you couldn't answer 'yes' to any of these, then you have a long way to go. Even the most old-fashioned organisations set goals for themselves, so it is probable that most organisations have some form of standards culture. The variation between them is purely a matter of degree.

To achieve a truly performance-based culture, standards need to be introduced, understood by everyone, worked towards and often exceeded, and measured as a matter of course. Although you may be a long way from this position now, achieving a standards culture is not difficult – it is more a matter of will, than of way.

BUILDING ON YOUR EXPERIENCE

An organisation with a standards culture is one in which all employees:

- know why they are there and the contribution expected of them
- can tell you their last month's/quarter's/year's performance figures over which they have a direct effect
- know what they have to do to achieve their target performance
- can describe or show you the standards to which they work
- can tell you about other organisations in the same business and say how they match them.

To build a culture like this, you will need to embrace the language of performance and the concepts of:

- performance specification
- objective assessment
- continuous measurement and review.

THE LANGUAGE OF PERFORMANCE

In this book, we are concentrating on the particular benefits of adopting national standards, but it is important to consider for a moment how other performance indicators differ from national standards.

Everyone uses the language of measurement in a slightly different way, but, one way or another, an organisation with a standards culture is probably familiar with these concepts:

- Goals (define the general direction in which we should be heading)
- *Performance Indicators* (define the critical areas in which success can be measured)
- *Targets* (set out an actual number and timescale within the critical area)
- *National Standards* (define good practice which enables the target to be met).

So, for example, in an organisation concerned with improving its equal opportunities practice, we might see the following in place:

- *Goal:* to improve equality of opportunity within this organisation
- *Performance Indicator:* the number of industrial tribunal decisions upheld against us
- *Targets:* two or less this year, none from next year on
- National Standards: see the set developed by the Employment Occupational Standards Council for Personnel Professionals covering:
  - Promoting equality of opportunity
  - Designing and selecting processes for monitoring and facilitating equal opportunities
  - Communicating and gaining support for equal opportunities practices
  - Monitoring and evaluating equal opportunities practices.

In this example of achieving true equality, the national standards add 'how' to 'what'. We have not included the entire national standard for equal opportunities because it runs to several pages, but it covers all the essential aspects of running an effective equal opportunities policy in an organisation.

WHERE DO YOU GET HOLD OF NATIONAL STANDARDS?

If national standards are so useful, why, you may ask, can't I buy a set in Asda? Unfortunately, there is no central distribution point for national standards. You cannot buy them from a high street retailer. The government department which funded their development has devolved responsibility for them to lead bodies, and each lead body either makes them available or passes enquiries on to the awarding bodies for the relevant qualifications or a handling agent. A very messy picture.

However, those standards which are fully developed are all recorded in two places: the NCVQ *Database of National Standards* and the Kogan Page *British Vocational Qualifications Directory*.

Because some of the standards you may want to use are not quite fully developed, and not yet in either of these places, you may have to contact the relevant lead body who will tell you what stage of development the draft standards are in and whether or not you can have a draft copy. (Offering to comment on them or take part in field trials can often win you a copy.)

The people who will be able to point you in the right direction are the NVQ/SVQ officers at your local TEC or LEC.

HOW DO YOU EMBED NATIONAL STANDARDS?

Once you get hold of a copy of the relevant national standards, you can begin to think about how they could be useful in your HR systems.

If you are a green field site, you will probably be able to start at the top of the job cycle and begin by embedding standards into recruitment, then move on to training and development, performance management, reward, and finally release and redeployment.

Figure 4.1 HR processes

If you are a brown field site, our experience has shown that it might be best if you started with your performance management system. Build standards first into agreed performance expectations, begin appraising people after a period of time, then the training and development, reward, and other HR processes should follow naturally.

In Chapter 2, we described how, in the absence of a set of standards, organisations currently struggle with these HR processes. What now follows suggests in detail how you can embed standards into HR as painlessly as possible.

EMBEDDING STANDARDS INTO RECRUITMENT PROCESSES

The trouble with job descriptions is ...

Every recruiter needs to get hold of, or to write, a specification which describes the job or the role on offer. Typically, it will describe the main duties, responsibilities and tasks required. Occasionally it will include additional information such as budget, terms and conditions. The following job description contains much of the information you would normally expect to find on a job description. As an example, we have taken the role of office manager in a professional services firm.

TITLE: Office Manager	DEPARTMENT: X
REPORTS TO: Partner X	BASED AT: XXX
PURPOSE OF THE JOB: To streamline and take over business activities so that consultants and partners can charge more time to clients.	
MAIN JOB OBJECTIVES: To 1 maintain the building fabric, services, equipment and supplies 2 provide secretarial and administrative support to consultants and partners 3 provide facilities for non-routine documents and non-routine data analysis 4 maintain the firm's management information system 5 recruit and manage temporary and permanent administrative staff	

STAFF REPORTING TO JOB:
    Administrative Assistant
    Temporary administrative staff
	ANNUAL BUDGET: X
	OTHER RESOURCES: X

OTHER INTERNAL RELATIONSHIPS: Consultants, Partners	
EXTERNAL RELATIONSHIPS: Clients, Suppliers, Professional Advisers (Surveyors, Accountants, Solicitors)	
TERMS OF EMPLOYMENT: Full-time, 25 days holiday, basic salary plus profit-related bonus	

Figure 4.2 Job description for office manager

This looks comprehensive, but what this document lacks is any kind of statement of what is really expected: what will be frowned upon, what will be smiled at, what will enable the people to whom the individual reports to say 'Yes, she's doing very well'. In fact, what is lacking is any qualitative description of how well the job needs to be done. In other words, standards.

Taking the example, Figure 4.2, success in the five activities listed could be measured by the following standards.

Figure 4.3 Job description for office manager enhanced with standards

TASKS	Performance Standards
1 Maintenance of facilities	
• the building	the fabric is not allowed to deteriorate noticeably without being repaired/renewed
• services	they continue without interruption
• equipment	hardware is not allowed to malfunction without being repaired
	software is upgraded when new versions become available
	new hardware and software is recommended where it could potentially benefit the business
• supplies	supplies are replenished before they run out
2 Provision of secretarial/administrative support	
• post inwards	mail received daily is opened first thing in the morning and as soon as possible after the midday delivery
	all incoming mail is date stamped, sorted and distributed to the appropriate people
	parcel and courier deliveries are accepted when necessary, and goods checked and signed for
• post outwards	mail is collected daily by 4.30pm where possible
	envelopes and packaging are suitable for the size and weight of the documents
	all items are weighed and stamped as required, and addressee and company names recorded in the Post Book
	postage rate and method is determined by the degree of urgency and/or cost (1st Class, Special Delivery, Data Post, courier, etc..)
	mail is posted in time for collection by the Post Office or taken to the counter as necessary
	stamps are bought before they run out, and filed and sorted in the Stamp Book
• telephone	calls are answered after no more than two rings
	callers are welcomed by tone of voice, and referred or dealt with appropriately
	messages are written clearly, put in message book and passed on when recipients call in

• *visitor care*	*visitors are made welcome by behaviour and by attendance to their needs*
• *arranging travel and meetings in association with consultants*	*arrangements enable travellers to use their time efficiently* *arrangements take account of the financial contexts of the projects or activities*
• *maintain partnership records (paper and computer-based)*	*records are organised and labelled with sufficient clarity for an interested third party to locate any document*
	backlog of filing does not exceed one day
• *maintaining project records*	*as for partnership records*

3 Production

• *WP/DTP*	*consultants' and partners' production of their own routine WP is supported by the provision of job aids (eg templates) advice and guidance*
	designs for non-routine documents are adapted (in negotiation with the originators) to make the WP/DTP involved as simple as possible without reducing the documents' effectiveness
	deadlines for non-routine documents are arranged (in negotiation with the originators) to the extent possible to smooth workflow
	non-routine documents conform to house style and are completed to schedule
• *reprographics*	*reprographic methods are chosen to give the quality required at the least cost (including the Officer Manager's time at £X per hour, Administration Assistant's time at £X per hour, and temporary staff time at cost)*
	clarity of reproduction and accuracy of collation are confirmed before documents are dispatched
• *data processing*	*methods of data processing (including choice/purchase of software) are determined (in association with the originator) to make the entry and analysis as simple as possible while achieving the outputs required*
	deadlines for data processing are arranged (in negotiation with originator) to the extent possible to smooth workflows
• *data processing*	*data processing is completed to schedule*

4 *Management Information System* (To be completed by firm's accountant)
- *time records*
- *management information*
- *payroll*
- *debit & credit control*
- *PAYE, NI & VAT*
- *bookkeeping*

5 *Staff management*

• *liaison between administrative staff, and consultants and partners*	consultants and partners are kept informed of administrative workloads and responsibilities (through diary meetings)
	administrative staff are warned of impending additional work to enable them to plan their workflows (through diary meetings)
	misunderstandings between consultants and partners, and administrative staff are resolved or referred to a partner
• *managing administrative staff*	responsibilities, objectives and, if necessary, methods of work are agreed with colleagues
	performance of colleagues is monitored to form the basis of constructive feedback
	difficulties or disputes are resolved with, if necessary, the support of a partner
• *recruiting temporary administrative staff*	arrangements are made to recruit temporary staff before crises develop
	unsuitable temporary staff are rejected as soon as their weaknesses become apparent
	suitable temporary staff are used to ease workflows as overall budgets or project budgets allow
• *recruiting permanent administrative staff*	new posts are recommended where they could potentially benefit the business
	job descriptions and person specifications for new posts are developed, and are agreed with partners
	recruitment procedures are recommended to partners and implemented when agreed
	first, second and (possibly) third choice applicants are recommended to partners for their final approval

Figure 4.3 Job description for office manager enhanced with standards

Yes, there's a lot here. But we wanted to show you how each of the activities can be enhanced with the addition of standards which can be objectively measured. Although these standards are not national standards, they were derived from national standards and reflect the same principles.

The advantage of using standards in recruitment

We strongly recommend the effort required to attach standards to a job or role description. In our experience it pays off again and again for those who are hiring and those who are being hired. In fact, an experience we had with one of our clients illustrates the recruit's viewpoint very well.

Case study

The client was a small medical equipment manufacturing company on the South coast. They were doing well and needed to expand their team to include the new post of Marketing Manager. As we had been working with them for a while developing standards with their top managers, they asked us to draw up standards for the new role (they called them 'enhanced job descriptions'). The national standards were not available at that time, so we developed a set with them.

Without telling us, they put these standards into the recruitment pack which they sent to job applicants, along with information about the company, terms and conditions. When we heard this, we expressed a concern that the candidates may feel this information was a little premature. What's more, the standards ran to nearly ten pages and we thought it might put potential recruits off.

However, the appointment was finally made, and when we got a chance we asked the new Marketing Manager what she thought of the information pack she had been sent and the set of standards for her job in particular. Her response was that she was intrigued, and all the more keen to work for a company that took her performance requirements so seriously that they were prepared to spell them out so clearly. What's more, she claimed that she had a greater understanding of the job when she started on Day 1.

Specifying requirements for selection

So, the first stage in any job cycle is specifying the job role and the standards by which success in the job should be measured. The second stage is selecting people against those standards.

Now it can be very difficult in a selection interview to ascertain whether or not a candidate could meet a set of standards. For a start, the candidate is not currently in the job, so any estimate of his or her future performance is hypothetical. Nonetheless, it is the role of the recruiter to envisage that hypothetical situation, imagine the candidate within it and assess how well the candidate would be able to meet the relevant standards.

The standards can be useful in three ways here: as a guide for the design of assessment centres, as a reminder during interview of the expectations for successful candidates, and as a guide for the candidate to help them prepare for the interview.

To help prevent any dispute during recruitment, or a selection case going as far as an industrial tribunal, if both the applicant and the organisation recruiting understand the standards to be met, then each should be able to justify their claims and understand the decisions made.

Using standards in simulated exercises

Those who use simulated assessments to select staff are usually looking to take the essentials of the job in question and distil them into a series of exercises. A set of standards gives the designer a list of the critical activities to simulate and a set of criteria by which success can be measured.

Taking our example of the office manager, a short simulated exercise could be designed where, for example, the office manager returns from holiday to find urgent messages about the building, services, equipment and supplies to which the candidate must respond. The quality of his or her response can be compared to the standards listed above.

Case study

As a real example, a few years ago we were faced with an interesting challenge from a client who needed to change the type of person traditionally recruited into a role. English Heritage, recently privatised, had previously recruited custodians for their national monuments often from the ranks of retired police officers, military personnel and others with similar backgrounds. This was because such people were well equipped to deal with the security aspects of the job, and to ensure that visitors to the site did not damage the fabric of the building or monument and followed the instructions to 'stay off the grass', etc.

With privatisation and a general up-dating of image, the need for a new type of custodian evolved: one who could welcome visitors, give guided tours, sell membership of English Heritage, as well as keep the building and its inhabitants (often animals) secure and undamaged.

English Heritage asked us to develop a set of standards for the new job and to help them find the right kind of people. This meant recruiting from a different pool to the one they were familiar with. Additionally, because the new pool would include people who might not have previously carried out a custodial role, we had to develop simulations of the custodian's role to see how they would cope with typical situations if they were appointed to the job.

The standards included:

- Care of the property
  - preparing and opening the property
  - closing the property
  - housekeeping
  - maintaining the grounds
  - keeping animals
- Care of visitors
  - visitor reception and departure
  - pre-arranged visits
  - guiding
  - health, safety and security responsibilities
- Internal management
  - records and returns
  - assisting in the running of events
  - working in a team
  - leading a team
- Promoting the work of English Heritage
  - displaying merchandise
  - selling merchandise
  - promoting membership of English Heritage.

With standards in these areas, we were able to design a number of exercises, including:

- A brief test of candidates' ability to classify and calculate the cheapest form of admission fee for a family, a coach party and individuals of different ages and circumstances

- A group exercise designed to see how well they responded to a suspected fire
- A test of their ability to remember and provide historical information about the monument
- A role play exploring the candidates' ability to handle complaints from visitors.

The last exercise was assessed using the following standards:

- The candidate used a polite greeting
- Speech was clear and sufficiently loud for the circumstances
- Friendly body language and eye contact was used to help communication
- The candidate remained calm and confident during the conversation
- The candidate elicited the visitors' difficulty, listened to their needs, clarified misunderstandings, and showed concern
- The result of the conversation ensured both the visitors' safety and enjoyment and the security of the monument.

You may ask why go to so much trouble to recruit a custodian. The cost of recruiting and training a new custodian, and the cost of the damage to public relations which a poor custodian can do, far outweigh the trouble taken in recruiting good custodians in this way.

Using standards in a selection interview

Even if you're not going to the extent of designing assessment exercises, you will probably be interviewing candidates. Having a description of the role and standards at your elbow during a selection interview can remind the interviewer of the key tasks in the role and the requirements which the applicant would be expected to meet. Careful questioning can then ascertain whether the candidate can complete the kind of tasks that meet your standards.

Illustration

For example, in the course of an interview for a computer services supervisor, the recruiter may be trying to ascertain how well the candidate would be able to *train and support users*.

The national standard in this area describes how to help users remember to back up their data and help them to recover data they have lost. The standards include the following performance criteria:

- The vulnerability of data and the necessity to maintain back-up copies and security of data and media is clearly explained

- Established back-up procedures and disciplines are clearly explained to the user
- User is made aware of existing back-up facilities of network
- Requirements to back-up own files which are not centrally maintained are explained
- Central back-up schedule is explained
- Back-ups carried out on a regular and irregular basis and checks and controls on storage carried out centrally are explained clearly
- The user is treated with tact and courtesy and is checked to have understood procedures and to be able to carry them out.

If you were interviewing the candidates and using the standard above, you could ask them what needs to be explained to a user, and to describe an incident when they had to help someone who had lost data.

Finally, if during the interview you are skilful enough to ascertain training needs, then the standards can act as a focus for induction, as described in the next section.

Using standards to prepare for an interview

If the standards for the job are shared with candidates prior to their interview, candidates can use the standards they have been sent to identify a piece of evidence to bring to the interview that would demonstrate how they have met standards previously. In our example of the office manager, a payroll system they have designed may be appropriate.

EMBEDDING STANDARDS INTO TRAINING AND DEVELOPMENT

The trouble with objectives is …

One of the great strengths of having something clearly laid out in terms of performance is that you are close to having the ideal training objectives. As most people will agree, the objectives you are trying to achieve are the first things to establish when you begin any kind of training or development. However, the problem with most training objectives is that they tend to be self-fulfilling; that is, they simply aim at what the trainer is trying to do, and not what the learner should end up doing as a result of the training or development. For example, a typical induction training objective might be to introduce new recruits to the organisation.

Such an objective would involve describing the organisation's history, business, products, services and geography. However, this objective will, in all likelihood, be achieved, because it describes precisely what the trainer is doing, rather than the improved performance of the learner.

Continuing our example, better objectives might be:

- for new recruits to be able to describe the organisation's history, business, main products and services
- for new recruits to be able to find their way around the site to all major departments without having to ask for directions.

So, in summary, good learning objectives should describe the ultimate performance which the training or development is trying to achieve.

Using standards in training objectives

This is where standards come in, because not only do they describe the ultimate performance, but they provide measures of success. So standards can be helpful in both laying out the intended outcomes of training from the learner's point of view, and in providing the wherewithal to evaluate training programmes. For example, let us suppose that our office manager is being given some training in recruiting temporary staff. The standards say:

- arrangements are made to recruit temporary staff before crises develop
- unsuitable temporary staff are rejected as soon as their weaknesses become known
- suitable temporary staff are used to ease workflows as overall budgets or projects allow.

The training would therefore need to aim at ensuring the efficient use of temporary staff. By using the standards, the trainer knows that the office manager doesn't need to be able to describe the recruitment procedure, or to use a specified method of recruitment, but simply to use temporary staff to manage the required quantity and quality of work.

Sticking with this example, we also know that if:

- crises develop before temps are recruited, or
- unsuitable temps are not rejected when their weaknesses become known, or
- temps are recruited when the budget does not allow,

then something has gone wrong and, possibly, it was caused by poor training.

The situation is exactly the same for personal development, even at a very senior level. For example, encouraging professionals such as architects, engineers or surveyors to continue their own professional development is a thorny issue among the large multidisciplinary construction practices.

The human resource team in a large practice would be looking to develop their mid-career professionals by encouraging them to keep up to date, attend conferences, build their portfolio of expertise, and so on. Furthermore, what distinguishes these people as professionals is that they should be tackling major decisions, concerning complex problems, and maybe even ethical matters.

The national standards in this area include:

- Exchange information and provide advice on matters of technical concern
- Identify, reframe and generate solutions to complex, indeterminate problems
- Contribute to the protection of individual and community interests.

So development programmes for professionals should include exposure to these areas, and progress can be evaluated on how well the individual is meeting the standards.

EMBEDDING STANDARDS IN PERFORMANCE MANAGEMENT

By now you will be getting the picture that a set of standards can act as the focal point for many HRD activities, and performance management is no different. If we take the performance management cycle as being composed of the activities here, then of course you can manage performance without a set of standards. However, we hope to demonstrate how much more effective performance management can be if you use standards.

Figure 4.4 Standards as the focal point for performance management

Appraisal processes

An organisation which appraises people without standards is probably using a combination of headings such as accountabilities, key result areas, competence, and is probably rating people on a scale of 1–5 against performance in these areas. This is rather like a draughtsman checking a drawing with a ruler which has no marks on it.

An organisation which appraises people with standards is using the tools above, but with clearly defined marks against which to compare performance. Imagine how much easier and how much more helpful it is to appraise someone with Model B than with Model A below.

MODEL A: PERFORMANCE REVIEW WITHOUT STANDARDS

NAME: A N Other

POSITION: Accounts Manager

OBJECTIVE: Plan new general ledger system

REVIEW OF PERFORMANCE: Ms Other has not achieved this objective

MODEL B: PERFORMANCE REVIEW WITH STANDARDS

NAME: A N Other
POSITION: Accounts Manager
OBJECTIVE: Plan new general ledger system
STANDARD:
by 31 August
Set and update objectives for the implementation team
- *Objectives are clear, accurate, and contain all relevant details including measures of performance*
- *Achievement of objectives is practicable within the set period, given other work commitments*
- *Objectives are explained in sufficient detail and in a manner, and at a level and pace appropriate to all the relevant individuals*
- *Objectives are updated regularly with the relevant individuals to take into account individual, team and organisational changes*
- *Individuals are encouraged to seek clarification of any areas of which they are unsure.*
Plan activities of the implementation team
- *The degree of direction required by individuals is accurately assessed and used to best effect in overall work planning*
- *Relevant views are sought in a way that encourages each individual to offer suggestions*
- *Where possible, decisions on work methods include suggestions from those involved*
- *Work methods and activities are consistent with current management priorities, organisational objectives and legal requirements and include opportunities for individual development wherever possible*
- *Work methods and activities optimise the use of available material, capital and people*
- *Where legal requirements and organisational development objectives conflict, the problem is identified and advice sought from appropriate people*
- *Agreed work methods and activities are designed to ensure that organisational objectives are achieved.*

REVIEW OF PERFORMANCE:
Ms Other did not achieve this standard or this deadline. The main reasons were that:
- *the objectives she set were not as clear as they might have been and unrealistic for new staff*
- *the amount of direction she needed to give X was underestimated*
- *she could not plan the methodology because of the ongoing IT system review (ie, not her fault).*

Perhaps Model B is a little more cumbersome than Model A, but it lets Ms Other know exactly what she needs to do next time to put things right. Model A on the other hand, leaves a whole load of questions unanswered. 'Why didn't she achieve it?' 'What should she do next time?' 'Was it due to inadequacies in her performance?' With Model B, you are obliged to have discussions about performance. They need not be as negative as the example; in fact, going into this much detail on the standards reinforces good practice.

MANAGING PEOPLE'S PERFORMANCE

It is not only the process of appraisal that benefits from the clarity which standards bring, but all aspects of managing performance.

- Agreeing expectations
- Measuring performance
- Analysing performance shortfalls, etc.

By way of illustration, we have developed a performance management algorithm which we call the Management Maze (see Figure 4.5, Solutions to performance problems, on page 54) and, as you've guessed, it relies on standards as anchor for performance. The Management Maze is useful because it does not presume that a performance problem surfaces because of one simple reason. It investigates what that reason might be. The typical causes of performance problems are:

- the task is too difficult and needs to be reorganised
- there was a communication breakdown over exactly what was required
- the person was not willing to do it, or to do it in that way
- the person was not able to do it, or to do it in that way.

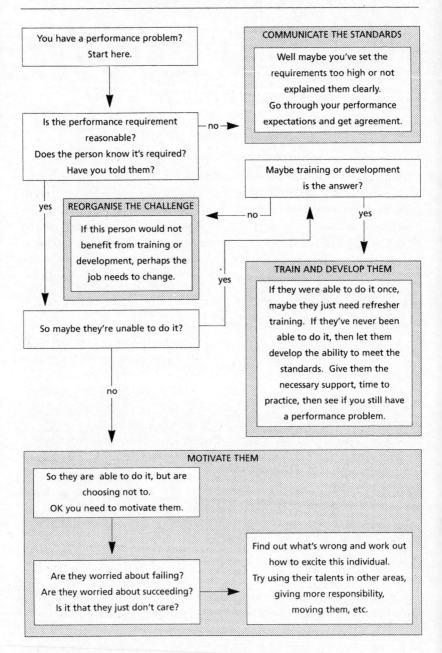

Figure 4.5 Solutions to performance problems (The Management Maze)

The Management Maze helps sort out what type of performance problems are occurring and suggests solutions.

- Reorganise the challenge so it's more realistic
- Ensure that the person fully understands the challenge and the standards to be met
- Encourage, motivate, empower the person so he or she is willing to face the challenge
- Train, develop and enable the person to meet the challenge.

Central to the Management Maze and to sorting out the performance problem is the use of standards. If you are using a set of standards, then your definition of requirements is likely to be clear, your appraisal is likely to be more objective and less contentious, your training and development is likely to be more focused and more objectively assessed and your evaluation of performance and subsequent reward is likely to be easier to manage.

EMBEDDING STANDARDS IN REWARD MANAGEMENT

The successful management of reward depends to a large degree on sorting out the basics. Once your reward philosophy is in place, spelling out clearly what you believe reward is for, what you as an organisation are prepared to pay for, and how you believe reward should change people's behaviour, then you can develop reward policies, processes and systems.

Typically, if your reward philosophy has linked pay to performance, the measures used to describe that performance will include:

- hard, quantifiable measures such as financial targets
- soft, qualifiable measures such as objectives or non-numerical targets
- ratings based on how well the individual has displayed a set of behaviours or has a set of competencies
- ratings based on how well the individual has met a set of performance criteria.

The first two give rise to fairly unequivocal agreement between raters and those rated: either the thing was done or not, the sales were achieved, the deadline was met.

The second two, because they are based on considered opinion, rely quite heavily on the rigour and clarity with which the descriptors or indicators of performance are written. Poorly written descriptors can give rise to contention and, where money is concerned, that can become quite troublesome.

This is where standards come in. A set of standards results from lots of people thinking very hard about the critical aspects of performance and the key measures of success, and writing them down so they are unambiguous. This takes time and effort, more time and effort than you may wish to allow. National standards therefore may offer useful criteria on which to base your performance ratings for reward purposes.

There is a final and very important reason for considering national standards in designing performance-related pay measures. Performance is a funny thing; what gets measured, gets done, they say. The obvious example which springs to mind is of the salesman who concentrates all his attention on achieving sales targets and neglects his paperwork, steals customers from colleagues, and generally creates mayhem around him. But he achieves his targets.

Targets are usually set annually, quarterly or within some specific time frame, because they reflect some specific activity that has to be achieved. They are, if you like, the annuals of the performance garden. Standards, on the other hand, reflect good practice. They describe what standards an individual in that occupation or profession should always be achieving, in any or every activity. You can think of these as the perennials in the performance garden. A good reward system should reward both annual and perennial achievement.

For example, companies increasingly concerned about standards of customer service are employing 'mystery shoppers' to assess their front desk staff. Barclays Bank send bogus customers to their tellers' windows on a regular basis and assess their tellers' response against standards. In addition, the tellers are assessed through their performance management system against objectives. There you have it: the annual and perennial sides of performance.

RELEASE AND REDEPLOYMENT

Finally, having travelled through a complete job cycle from recruitment onwards, we arrive at the point at which decisions have to be made to end the appointment. This may be at the request of the job holder, perhaps because he or she wants to leave or to accept voluntary redundancy, or it could be because the organisation is requesting that the person leaves, as in the case of enforced redundancy or dismissal.

If someone resigns from a position of their own accord, then standards are fairly irrelevant (except in that they will be of great help in writing this person a reference). However, if the organisation needs to make a decision about the person's future with the organisation, or to offer them redeployment within the organisation, then standards can help in:

- identifying candidates on the basis of fairness
- supporting the organisation's need to dismiss someone on the grounds of poor performance, through appraisal records, assessments against standards, etc
- helping identify suitable redeployment opportunities by looking at the enhanced job descriptions and standards with a potential job mover.

In the words of Tony Miles, of Glaxo Wellcome, 'When we hire staff or reshuffle staff who have the relevant NVQ, we feel confident that they're up to the job.'

RECOMMENDATIONS

The chapter has looked at where you start if you want to embed standards into your recruitment, training and development, performance management, reward, release and redeployment systems. If it seems like a good idea, consider how far your current culture is from the description of an organisation where standards are a way of life:

- get hold of a set of relevant national standards
- look through the national standards to understand how they could add value to your HR processes
- begin by planting the standards into your performance expectations for this role
- if you have no-one yet in this role, then recruit them on the basis of the standards
- if you already have individuals in this role, then introduce the standards to them and agree how they will be embedded into their performance management processes
- develop the approach into
  - training and development
  - reward
  - release and redeployment processes.

5 HOW TO IMPORT NATIONAL STANDARDS WITHOUT LOSING THEIR VALUE

CHAPTER SUMMARY

It will have become quite apparent by now that national standards are very comprehensive and full of useful detail. Unfortunately, this makes them cumbersome to use easily in HR processes. Although for the purposes of NVQs and SVQs, national standards are used in their undiluted form, the standards in everyday use within HR systems could be modified.

There are obviously certain dangers in tampering with a set of national standards, so this chapter shows how you might modify them for your own purposes, without losing their value or their integrity.

The method

When you see your first set of national standards, pause before pronouncing judgement! They look cumbersome at first sight. They may even appear unintelligible. There are very good reasons why national standards look as they do, and you need to know what they are.

The national standards have been written by groups of people who know the occupation well and who can represent those who are in this occupation. Typically, those groups will have been led by consultants who are specialists in the standards methodology. Once written, the standards will have been taken from the originators and sent to a large number of people (usually 500–1000) for comment. They will then have been redrafted and tested out in the field for the purposes of assessing people against the standard. If the standards are too high or too low, or too difficult to understand, they will be revised again and then sent to the Lead Body for approval.

All national standards are derived by a process called functional analysis. This method was chosen for the national standards programme because:

- it describes activities in terms of outcomes rather than processes, which means that variations in methods are accommodated, and the concentration is on results
- it captures all the critical aspects of the work role
- it doesn't specify technology in detail, so the standards don't need to be updated when the technology changes.

The method is very rigorous and undoubtedly can produce a fine quality product. But it is very hard to do functional analysis well. For many people, it is an unnatural process. It is intellectually challenging and full of pitfalls. For example, you can end up with a result which looks to be intellectually correct but which means little to the occupation it is supposed to describe.

The language

By far the biggest gripe among those who use national standards is that the language is turgid, often to the point of being unintelligible. There is no doubt that many sets of standards are dense with information, and sometimes the sheer length of them puts people off, even if that length is packed with quality. However, it is true that some are badly presented, which doesn't help, and others are just poorly written.

The problem has come about, we believe, because of a conflict of purpose. National standards are at one and the same time intended to:

- describe good practice in an occupation
- provide a tool for valid and reliable assessment.

If they were only there to describe good practice, they would be written in a way that is helpful, user-friendly and full of additional information and supporting notes. But, more usually, the need to be a useful assessment tool overrides their user-friendliness. As a consequence they are often written in a way that ensures they capture all relevant requirements, thereby making them very dense with information, and difficult to understand without two or three readings.

Although very often users will take several attempts to untangle the various parts of a standard, once they have understood what the originators intended, they agree with the way it has been expressed and find they cannot or do not wish to change it. An excellent way of becoming familiar with the standards is to use them practically in the workplace to plan or carry out assessments.

THE CHANGES YOU MAY WANT TO MAKE

You may feel that given such difficulties, you couldn't possibly use national standards in your HR processes, without making substantial modifications. You may feel you need to:

- reduce the number of standards by leaving some out
- reduce the number of performance criteria

- reduce the range
- contextualise the standards for your environment
- distil the essence of the standards into a shorter list
- rewrite them completely.

Let's look at the implications of making such changes.

QUALITIES YOU RISK LOSING

If you simplify the wording of the standards you risk losing precision, assessability and access to a national framework against which to judge performance. This may be of no consequence and, if so, go ahead.

Reducing the standards: units and elements

If you reduce the number of standards, you will be losing a part of the occupation because each standard defines an important outcome of that occupation. If the people concerned are not responsible for that outcome in their job, then it may not matter to you. For example, the units for pensions administrators include activities such as:

- provide pensions information on request
- determine retirement benefits
- determine death benefits,
- providing training in pensions administration

Most pensions administrators will not get involved in training. However, whilst the individuals concerned may not be currently employed to carry out training, they may want very much to be competent to train because their future career depends on it.

Reducing the standards: performance criteria

If you cut out performance criteria, you will be missing out on good practice and on the critical aspects of doing a job well.

Reducing the standards: the range

If you reduce the range, then you will be losing vital breadth of competence. However, in a particular firm you might not need all of the range.

CONTEXTUALISING THE STANDARDS

If you contextualise the standards so they make sense for your environment, you don't risk losing a lot. The best examples we have seen of contextualised standards are those which annotate the published page with explanations for the particular environment. This has the advantage of leaving the national standard unaltered. For example, the following standard drawn from the set produced by Management Charter Initiative (MCI) has been contextualised for the legal profession. The standard is about how to work in collaboration with others. The left-hand side shows the Management Charter Initiative (MCI) standard and the right hand side shows the Law Society's guidance on how to use the standard in legal practice.

MCI STANDARD

WORKING IN COLLABORATION: *Identify and set up collaborative and consultative working arrangements.*		RELEVANCE *Use this standard if you are interested in*
PERFORMANCE CRITERIA • *Collaborative and consultative working arrangements are explored and set up where programmes, projects and plans would benefit from them.* • *Collaborative and consultative working arrangements are adequately resourced.* • *Participants are inducted and trained both in the ways of working and in the backgrounds and expectations of their partners.* • *Targets, objectives, standards and values are consistent across the partners.* • *Where difficulties in collaboration and consultation occur, support is provided to help partners find ways which remain consistent with the organisation's requirements.*	RANGE *Collaboration and consultative approaches may be needed for technical or for values/policy reasons.* *These may be organised within and between teams, departments, units and organisations, up to an international level. They may include external organisations.* *Resources required may include:* • *travel* • *transport* • *telecommunications* • *physical environments.* *Collaboration may be:* • *large scale* • *small scale* • *short term* • *long term.*	• *working with or consulting your peers within the practice on particular matters.* • *working with or consulting staff at an equivalent level in other organisations on particular matters.* *But do not use this standard if you are interested in* • *delegating work to subordinates (this is addressed by standard C2.2).* MEANINGS *In this standard, the term* • *'collaborative working arrangement' refers to two or more parties working together for the same purpose: for example, three fee earners working on the same file, or the practice working together with a firm of accountants on an acquisition* • *'consultative working arrangement' refers to one party becoming available to advise another; for example, a fee earner with non-contentious experience on property agreeing to advise a litigation fee earner on relevant matters, an external management consultant contracting to advise a managing partner on management development within the practice* • *'partners' in criteria c, d and e refers to the different parties involved in the collaborative or consultative arrangements rather than the partners who own the practice.* APPLICATION *You might apply this standard if you were going to work with consultants, expert witnesses or investigators or locums.* *The standard directs you to be clear of the costs and benefits which will accrue before setting up the arrangements; to take the trouble to set up the arrangements in such a way that all parties understand what is expected of them; and to be ready to clarify the misunderstandings which can cause difficulties in all such arrangements.*

NHS GUIDANCE

The NHS has produced a version of the MCI standards for managers and a very extensive guide on how to use the standards to improve NHS organisational effectiveness. The NHS version contains some minor alterations which customise the standards so they are more relevant to the environment and culture of the NHS. For example, they refer to patients rather than customers. Here is an extract explaining how the MCI's range indicators should be interpreted for those who manage operating theatres.

UNIT 1: Maintain and improve service and product operations	RANGE OF ACTIVITY
ELEMENT 1.1: Maintain operations to meet quality standards	Below are some examples illustrating what the range statements of this element mean within the context of an Operating Department.
RANGE INDICATORS	Services:
Operations are all those activities within the manager's line responsibility.	• high standards of health care to patient • safe conditions • co-ordination of technical support • provision of supplies • provision of trained staff • training of staff.
Sources of supply (suppliers) are both: • external organisations • internal departments/teams.	Supplies are: • sterile supplies • non-sterile supplies • linen • theatre equipment • drugs.
Supplies are: • material • equipment/technology • financial • sub-contractors/ consultants/agency staff • information.	Specifications are: • purchaser contracts/agreements • service contracts/agreements • budget constraints • audit standards • current regulations.
Communication with customers is carried out by means of: • correspondence • meetings • telephone conversations.	Factors which disrupt services are those affecting: • functioning and availability of equipment/ drugs in theatre • availability of theatre team members • availability of clinicians • availability of patients
Factors which disrupt operations are those affecting: • supply • operational resource • quality of materials.	• quality and quantity of consumables • communications within the organisation • normal planning of activity, including emergencies, urgent cases, fire, preparation for war and major incidents
Corrective actions are consistent with organisational policy and within budgetary constraints.	• time over-runs on operations.

WHAT YOU WILL GAIN BY CHANGING THE STANDARDS?

If you actually change the standard rather than explain it, you will gain a tailor-made description of essential good practice. Instead of cumbersome but precise language, you will gain user-friendly statements which describe in general what is required.

For example, the following standard is intended to help readers understand what getting on with your manager is all about. The first version is the national standard. The second is rewritten for the organisation.

NATIONAL STANDARD

Enhance productive working relationships with one's immediate manager.

1 Immediate manager is kept informed in an appropriate level of detail about activities, progress, results and achievements.
2 Information about problems and opportunities is clear, accurate and provided with an appropriate degree of urgency.
3 Information and advice on matters within the given area of responsibility are sought from immediate manager as necessary.
4 Unclear proposals are not accepted, the reasons are considered and, where appropriate, alternative proposals are put forward.
5 Where proposals are not accepted, the reasons are considered and, where appropriate, alternative proposals are put forward.
6 Where there are disagreements, efforts are made to avoid damaging the relationship with the immediate manager.
7 Ways of improving the relationship with the immediate manager are actively sought.
8 Requirements of job role are satisfied.
9 Activities are performed in a helpful and willing manner.

REWRITTEN STANDARDS

Get on with your manager.
1 You tell your manager everything he or she needs to know.
2 You draw particular attention to things that you believe are critical or urgent.
3 Your timing is impeccable.
4 Whenever you need help deciding what to do or how to go about it, you ask.

5   When you want something, you make your proposal, laying out clearly all the risks, costs and benefits.
6   If he or she says no, you find out why and try an alternative approach if necessary.
7   When you disagree with each other, you make a real effort to avoid any long term damage to the relationship.

Remember:

• you still have to do the job to the standards expected
• communication between you is two way
• from time to time you may disagree, but it shouldn't affect the relationship
• you'll need your manager's support when you want something.

Similarly, it is possible to condense the essence of national standards into something more digestible. The national standards in Personnel, for example, have several themes running through them which can be summarised and expressed quite simply. For example:

Identify the need or opportunity to improve what you do:

• any need you identify is pressing, any opportunity irresistable
• you have consulted with all the relevant people.

TO CHANGE OR NOT TO CHANGE?

The decision to adopt the national standards in their virgin glory or to adulterate them rests with you. It depends to a very large degree on the amount of precision and breadth you require, and the quality of the national standards you are considering. If you want to use them simply as a general indicator of what is required, then change them. But be warned, the more you try to do, the more cumbersome you will find it. The more changes you make, the more you risk losing the benefits of the considerable thought that has gone into providing the standards in the first place.

If you need standards that are precise, for example for assessment, discipline or reward purposes, then don't change them. If you need to distil the standards because there are too many of them, for appraisal processes, for example, then lose the bulk but don't lose the essence. What you'll probably find yourselves doing, of course, is changing them into a friendly tool in order to get them accepted into the organisation, and then introducing the national standards as people become more familiar with the concept and ask for more precision.

RECOMMENDATIONS

We have laid out the advantages and disadvantages of playing around with national standards. If you are thinking of embedding the standards into your own HR processes:

- be selective in what you use and think twice before making any major changes;
- look over a set of national standards carefully, trying to understand what they mean; when you do, you will appreciate the rigour with which they have been prepared;
- equip the users of the standards in your organisation with the same depth of understanding about them as you have; if you stint here, you may be lost before you begin;
- if you have to contextualise the standards for your own environment, keep the national standards in tact and place your own interpretation of them on a facing page or in annotations;
- finally, if you want to rewrite them for yourselves, go ahead; break all the rules; but be aware that these alternatives will probably look and act more like guidance than proper standards.

We have told you in Part Two how you can use national standards to improve your HR processes by taking them lock, stock and barrel or even by taking liberties with them and embedding them into your culture.

If you want to take this further, by offering your employees a nationally recognised qualification, you will need to embrace NVQs and SVQs. In Part Three, we describe how to get into bed with an Awarding Body, develop the relationship and consummate the affair with the award of qualifications.

By now you should have an understanding of how standards can be used as tools to help organisations meet their business needs, by developing employees in an objective way. You may be at the point of thinking about how you can recognise achievement by awarding your employees with an NVQ or SVQ.

This part of the book provides you with guidance on what you will need to do to embed NVQs or SVQs into your organisation. To help you get the most out of the chapters here are some of the 'jargon' words used in the NVQ/SVQ system:

Approved assessment centre An organisation where assessment takes place.

Candidate A person who is working towards an NVQ/SVQ. An NVQ/SVQ candidate can be an employee of an organisation or an unemployed person who is assessed in a college environment.

Assessor The person who assesses the candidate. Assessors can be employees of the organisation or they can come into an organisation on a peripatetic basis.

Internal verifier The person responsible for the quality of the assessment process. Internal verifiers can be employees of the organisation or they can come into an organisation on a peripatetic basis.

External verifier The person responsible for the quality of what is happening at the assessment centre. External verifiers are appointed by the awarding bodies.

CHAPTER SUMMARY

In this first chapter we will explain the opportunities that will open up to you, how an organisation must meet the national criteria for centre approval and verification which is used to put in place procedures and systems for operating the NVQ/SVQ. We will describe how the requirements of an awarding body provide your organisation with a system for measuring, reviewing and evaluating progress and for benchmarking yourself against the best in the class.

If you have used standards internally, then you may have found it a lonely business. By running NVQs/SVQs, you should have the opportunity to network with a variety of people through the systems put in place by the awarding body.

THE MAIN PLAYERS

NCVQ and SCOTVEC in Scotland
accredit qualifications and the bodies who award them

Awarding Bodies award NVQs and SVQs
(eg BTEC, Open University, City & Guilds)

Centres deliver the qualifications
(eg companies, colleges, consortia of employees)

It is important to understand who the main players are. Candidates are registered with the awarding body through the local assessment centre for their qualifications. The assessment centre could be their employer or another organisation.

Figure 6.1 Who's who in NVQs/SVQs

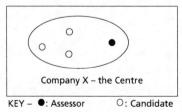

Company X – the Centre

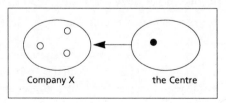

Company X   the Centre

KEY – ●: Assessor   O: Candidate

Figure 6.2 Candidates and assessors

SYSTEMS THAT SUPPORT CANDIDATES

Awarding bodies which offer NVQs or SVQs are required to make sure that centres have in place quality systems for operating the NVQ/SVQ. If anyone can simply set themselves up to offer NVQs/SVQs without approval from an awarding body, then collusion, corruption and unfair assessment is possible.

To help centres, NCVQ have published their national criteria for centre approval and verification criteria which describe the systems that centres must put in place to operate successful NVQs or SVQs.

The role of awarding bodies

As custodians of the national criteria for centre approval and verification, the awarding bodies are responsible for making sure that centres meet the national criteria. Organisations seeking to offer NVQs/SVQs have to prove to an awarding body that they can operate systems which meet the criteria.

It is worth remembering that the same NVQs and SVQs are often offered by more than one awarding body. Therefore, it is in your interest to work with the awarding body that provides you with the best service and most compatible systems. Our advice would be to choose an awarding body that not only provides advice, but actively helps you put in place the systems needed to run the NVQ or SVQ.

Awarding bodies should provide:

- a sympathetic telephone support service
- a consultancy service
- clear and well presented guidance and assessment materials
- an efficient and cost effective service.

After making a first enquiry you should feel confident that the awarding body is professional and responsive to your business needs. If it is not responsive, shop around.

Achieving quality

If you decide to become an assessment centre, you can expect the following.

- You will be required to prepare an application for centre approval by completing forms supplied by the awarding body.
- The application for centre approval will need to explain how you are going to operate an NVQ or SVQ by satisfying what is contained in the national criteria for centre approval and verification.

- You will need to forward your application for centre approval to the appropriate awarding body.
- The awarding body will normally forward your application to an external verifier who considers whether centre approval should be granted.
- If successful, centre approval is usually granted for three years.
- The external verifier will normally make two monitoring visits a year to the centre.

What you have to satisfy

If you find this all too much to cope with, then see if there is an approved centre near you which can help. Another centre may provide you with an assessor and internal verifier. In other words, ask whether you can tap into their existing system.

On the other hand, if you plan to become an assessment centre your application will be assessed against the following criteria for national centre approval and verification criteria:

Management systems

1   The centre specifies and maintains an effective system for managing NVQs/SVQs
   (i)   The centre has an explicit policy for promoting and implementing NVQs/SVQs
   (ii)   NVQ/SVQs' related roles, responsibility and authority are clearly defined
   (iii) A member of senior management formally approves the centre's agreement with the awarding body
   (iv)   The recording system design enables candidates' achievements to be evaluated in relation to the centre's equal opportunities policy
   (v)   Procedures are specified for communicating with senior management about the implementation of NVQs/SVQs
   (vi)   There are procedures for communicating within the NVQ/SVQ 'team'
   (vii) There are procedures for liaising with satellite and associated sites
   (viii) Resources required by candidates with special needs are identified and are made available

(ix) Procedures for maintaining and updating databases (IT or manual) are specified.

2 There are effective administrative arrangements
   (i)   Accurate records of the assessment of candidates are maintained
   (ii) Effective liaison with other assessment sites and associated organisations is maintained
   (iii) Awarding body administrative requirements are fulfilled promptly and correctly.

Staff resources

Staff resources are sufficient to deliver assessment for NVQs/SVQs
   (i)   Sufficient time is available to provide information, advice and counselling for all NVQ/SVQ candidates
   (ii)   There are sufficient competent and qualified assessors to assess for the qualification
   (iii) There are sufficient competent and qualified internal verifiers to ensure quality assessments
   (iv)   Internal verifiers have appropriate access to assessors
   (v)   Sufficient time is allowed for administering the programme
   (vi)   Staff development needs are systematically reviewed
   (vii) An NVQ/SVQ staff development programme is provided.

Assessment

A system for valid and reliable assessment to national standards is specified and maintained
   (i)   Information, advice and guidance on assessment are provided to NVQ/SVQ candidates and to potential NVQ/SVQ candidates
   (ii)   There is a system for co-ordinating assessment
   (iii) There is a system for reviewing the quality and fairness of the assessment process
   (iv)   There is an effective appeals procedure for candidates
   (v)   An appropriate range of assessment methods is used
   (vi)   Unit certification is available on demand.

Quality assurance and control

An effective system for quality assurance and control is maintained
   (i)   An effective system for quality assurance of assessment is in place

(ii) There are effective procedures for the internal verification of NVQs/SVQs

(iii) The quality of assessment is systematically reviewed and monitored.

Equal opportunities and access

There is clear commitment to equal opportunities

(i) There is an explicit policy on equal opportunities

(ii) Information, guidance and advice on equal opportunities is provided for new candidates, staff and work providers

(iii) There is an action plan for the implementation of the equal opportunities policy

(iv) Unit certification is available

(v) There is a system for monitoring and evaluating achievement rates of candidates in relation to equal opportunities

(vi) Requirements of special needs candidates for assessment are identified and met where possible.

BENEFITS OF MEETING THE CRITERIA

Even though the criteria may at first appear onerous, by jumping through the hoops you will find that they bring benefits to your organisation. The requirements will provide your organisation with a process for getting the work done, measuring, reviewing and evaluating progress against experience.

Using the criteria to benchmark your performance can in itself be a benefit, because you will be able to standardise the delivery of the NVQ/SVQ by working to clear guidelines, which will bring a focus to your work. In effect the criteria are a set of national standards.

SHARING EXPERIENCES

By being involved and joining the 'family' of other providers, you should have access to all sorts of networking arrangements. Your organisation will have opportunities to meet other people, share and compare ideas. By offering NVQs or SVQs you will be taking part in more formal structured arrangements. If you have used national standards internally, then access to other organisations may have been limited. Through the awarding body you are working with, you will come into contact with other organisations and people associated with NVQs/SVQs.

This involvement will provide you with opportunities to:

- share ideas
- solve problems
- exchange examples of good practice
- keep up to date with developments
- contribute to the success of the national standards movement.

Be prepared to share your ideas and systems with people from other organisations. If a particular activity is working well, then do not keep it to yourself. For example, if you have produced a brief guide for candidates on how the assessment system works, share this with other providers. They will probably be able to help you in other areas.

NETWORKING

To be honest, some awarding bodies are better than others at encouraging networking with other centres, but opportunities can come about through a variety of circumstances. Here are some examples.

- External verifiers will be responsible for several centres. They will have knowledge of how different organisations are using NVQs/SVQs. They will have examples of good practice and case studies. They can put you in touch with other people. They are able to advise and help you solve problems. They can provide you with feedback from other organisations and the latest awarding body developments.
- Some centres local to each other are forming self-help groups to help and support each other. A group of organisations who have the same external verifier may come together on a regular basis. A local college may arrange self-help groups for the various organisations it is working in partnership with. The awarding body may have regional networks in place that organisations new to NVQs/SVQs can join.
- Research projects are always being carried out to review the success of NVQs/SVQs. Your centre may be invited to take part. This may result in researchers coming in to interview staff in your organisation. This will provide you with a different perspective. You can also pick the researcher's brains. The researcher may put you in touch with contacts in other centres.
- The awarding body may organise conferences, workshops, seminars and surgeries to bring people together to discuss NVQs or SVQs. For example, the awarding body for the chemical and pharmaceutical industries holds annual user conferences, where

representatives from centres meet to share experiences or good practice.

- The awarding body may be reviewing the use of the national standards or the quality of their centre approval and verification procedures. You may be required to complete questionnaires or take part in interviews. The awarding body will be able to put you in touch with other people who perhaps do not share your particular concerns so that you can compare your feelings and findings.
- The industry lead body responsible for the standards may be reviewing the quality and relevance of the standards. You may be given the opportunity to join working parties with other people who have also used the standards.
- The local TEC or LEC may be organising events to promote NVQs/SVQs, Investors in People Award or Modern Apprenticeship. At these gatherings you will meet other people with whom you could network.

It is of course up to you whether you take advantage of these opportunities to network with other people from different organisations. But instead of waiting to be approached by awarding bodies, TECs, LECs and groups of consultants, it may be worth informing your external verifier that you would be willing to help develop the NVQ/SVQ movement further by taking part in outside activities.

Organisations new to NVQs/SVQs may be anxious at meeting other people because of the fear of exposing any weaknesses. No one likes to feel foolish or unknowledgeable about a subject. However, from our experience this problem need not be so acute if you bear in mind that successful organisations may be willing to share their experience with fledglings. Remember, they were previously in the same position.

WORKING WITH THE EXTERNAL VERIFIER

As your system for operating your NVQ/SVQ takes shape, the external verifier will be issuing regular reports that will include actions that must be carried out and implemented. Any actions that improve the operation of the NVQ/SVQ should be based on the centre's need to meet the centre approval and verification criteria.

Some awarding bodies may also require additional activities in their quality monitoring systems. For example, you may be required to issue regular progress reports in between monitoring visits.

It is important to establish a good working relationship with the external verifier. Ideally external verifiers should not be policing your systems. They should in fact be helping you to meet the criteria for centre approval and verification, so that you are running a quality system that supports NVQ/SVQ candidates. Their job is to identify any gaps in your current arrangements and set you action plans and target dates to plug the gaps. Your job is to produce evidence that the external verifier can use to assess the performance of your centre as an NVQ/SVQ provider. Providing that you work in partnership with your external verifier and use the centre approval and verification criteria constructively, your NVQ/SVQ should be successful. Therefore, the role of the external verifier is one of judge rather than policeman.

RECOMMENDATIONS

In order to take advantage of the opportunities that NVQs/SVQs bring, we recommended in this chapter that you:

- recognise how the national criteria for centre approval and verification are designed to establish your systems for operating the NVQ/SVQ
- take advantage of and learn from the awarding body's monitoring systems
- recognise how the national criteria for centre approval verification criteria can be used to
    - improve the management and administration of the NVQ/SVQ
    - make use of all the physical resources available to you
    - organise and develop your staff resources
    - develop your systems of assessment
    - put in place a system of quality assurance and control
    - gain a commitment to equal opportunities and access
- use every opportunity to network with other NVQ/SVQ providers, so that you can
    - benchmark your performance against what other organisations are doing
    - share and learn from each other's experiences
- should be prepared to share your ideas and examples of good practice with people from other organisations
- use and act on the advice of your external verifier
- establish a good working relationship with your external verifier.

7 GETTING STARTED

CHAPTER SUMMARY

Let us assume that your organisation wants to become an assessment centre for an NVQ/SVQ. At this stage there is much you can do to put in place your quality and cost-effective systems for operating the NVQ/SVQ.

We have provided you with a systematic approach for managing the preparation of your submission, which at the same time will introduce your staff to the NVQ/SVQ process. We will describe how to secure the support of senior management, and if appropriate your union representatives, identify staff who can take part, allocate people jobs and manage the preparation of your submission for the appropriate awarding body.

YOUR RESPONSIBILITIES

As a potential assessment centre you can do much to start the ball rolling. You will have to develop systems for operating the NVQ/SVQ in a way that supports candidates and satisfies the criteria for centre approval and verification. Remember, assessment is usually carried out by people employed in your organisation. The awarding body can provide you with the tools and support, but it cannot operate the NVQ/SVQ for you.

OUTSIDE HELP

The awarding bodies' rules, practical guides, procedures for gaining centre approval, procedures for monitoring the performance of centres, assessment documentation and the advice of the external verifier are all provided to help you. But NVQs/SVQs will only be as good as the people who operate them. Awarding bodies can teach you to swim; it is up to you whether you take advantage of their help and learn to swim on your own.

It is your organisation's responsibility to:

- plan your submission for centre approval
- prepare your submission for centre approval
- seek centre approval
- operate, manage and develop the NVQ/SVQ
- assess candidate performance

- develop the competence of internal verifiers and assessors
- review and evaluate progress and develop further the systems of operation
- make changes in the light of experience.

In addition, the local TEC in England and Wales or the local LEC in Scotland may be able to put you in touch with people to help you plan how to operate the NVQ/SVQ. They may also have funds available to help you train staff and put in place your systems for operating the NVQ/SVQ.

Tax relief also may be obtainable for registration fees for NVQs/SVQs and on the tuition fees for training programmes.

FIRST STEPS

To help you plan how you are going to operate the NVQ/SVQ and meet the criteria for centre approval and verification, what follows are suggestions on what you can practically do in these early stages.

Get the support of senior management

In our experience senior management must support the NVQ/SVQs. Senior managers can measure the business benefits they bring and recognise how employee development can improve the business.

The NVQ/SVQ is more likely to be a success if the people involved believe that senior managers want it to work. Internal verifiers, assessors and candidates should receive support and encouragement from senior management. They should not be made to feel totally responsible for the success of the NVQ/SVQ assessment programme. An atmosphere of co-operation should be created, where people work together to solve problems and rectify any mistakes. Mistakes are fine as long as lessons are learned from them.

At this stage managers can help by:

- deciding whether NVQs/SVQs should be adopted in the first place
- encouraging staff to get involved during these planning stages
- explaining what the business expects to gain from running an NVQ/SVQ programme
- explaining that they will expect to be kept up to date with progress.

Get support from unions

If you employ people who belong to a trade union, it is essential that union representatives understand the NVQ/SVQ programme. You will need to assure representatives that the NVQ/SVQ is voluntary and that those employees who do not want to take part will not be penalised. NVQs/SVQs must not affect employees' rights or levels of pay.

The TUC supports NVQs/SVQs and campaigns to improve both the quantity and the quality of training available to union members. Different unions are actively involved in the development of standards through the appropriate industry lead body.

In the chemical and pharmaceutical industries, the General Municipal and Boilermakers' Union and Transport and General Workers' Union have together produced a *Trade Union Negotiators' Guide to Process Qualifications in the Chemical and Pharmaceutical Industries*. This guide offers local negotiators guidance on how they can be fully involved in decisions about the introduction of NVQs/SVQs at company and plant level. The guide encourages negotiators to persuade organisations to take up NVQs/SVQs, push for quality training based on the national standards and take an active part in monitoring the quality of the NVQ/SVQ on offer.

Register your interest with the awarding bodies

First identify which of your employees would benefit from an NVQ/SVQ. Then find out if an NVQ/SVQ exists to suit these employees. Your local TEC or LEC has access to the NCVQ database that lists all the NVQs/SVQs available. The TEC or LEC may even have copies of the various awarding bodies' documentation. They can offer you advice on how to approach the awarding body and set up your NVQ/SVQ.

Once you approach the appropriate awarding body ask:

- for a list of their publications and guides that are available for the NVQ/SVQ
- for details on how their centre approval system operates
- whether you can visit centres who are already approved
- whether you can meet the external verifier
- for details on how they will monitor future performance
- whether there are any networks that you could tap into or local self-help groups you could join
- whether any conferences, workshops, seminars or surgeries are being planned.

UNDERSTAND FULLY WHAT IS REQUIRED

Because you will be responsible for the operation of the NVQ/SVQ it is essential that you understand the particular awarding body's procedures, systems and methods of assessment. This point cannot be overstated. In our experience some centres have had problems because they have not bothered to find out exactly what is required by the awarding body.

ESTABLISH A GROUP TO PREPARE THE SUBMISSION

If the application is prepared by one person in isolation then it will suffer from ivory tower syndrome. At a later date staff will need time to understand what systems have been put in place. Whereas, if the team of people responsible for the NVQ/SVQ design the systems of operation they will be more likely to take ownership. In addition, they will be able to review the systems at a later date and update them according to their experience.

Some organisations give this group the status of a steering group, where it is chaired by a senior manager. The group allocates jobs to other members of staff and plans how the procedures for operating the NVQ/SVQ will be designed. They agree a target date for the completion of the application for centre approval. A rigorous timetable can help focus the mind. Agree dates when the tools will be prepared. Agree dates when the planning group will meet to review, discuss progress and identify gaps.

Any group, regardless of its status, can be effective in helping to prevent the work drifting. The focus a group like this brings, means that the work in preparing the application for centre approval will be taken seriously and completed on time.

Identify staff who can help

The application for centre approval will need to explain how the NVQ/SVQ will be operated. Contributions can be made by:

Managers who can prepare, for example:

- a statement on the organisation's commitment to NVQs/SVQs
- an explanation on what the organisation expects to gain from NVQs/SVQs in terms of improved performance and improvement on the bottom line
- a statement on how the NVQ/SVQ is linked into the organisation's business plan.

Potential assessors and internal verifiers, who can, for example:

- identify routine work activities that can be used to assess candidates
- update working procedures and instructions
- establish their own staff development programme
- establish methods for recording candidate progress
- develop an appropriate range of assessment methods
- develop an appeals system for candidates.

Staff from the personnel and training departments, who can, for example:

- provide the secretarial and administrative back-up
- establish systems for making sure that all concerned have access to the awarding body's guidance and literature
- prepare job descriptions for internal verifiers and assessors
- prepare organisational charts showing the reporting lines for candidates, assessors, internal verifiers, management, the external verifiers and the awarding body.

Any tools for operating the NVQ/SVQ will demonstrate to the external verifier and the awarding body your serious commitment to NVQs/SVQs. The best tools are those that actually describe what you will be doing, and those that will actually be used to support the candidates, assessors and internal verifiers.

Identify your group of candidates

In order to meet NCVQ's and SCOTVEC's open access policy, NVQs/SVQs must be open to anyone regardless of age, gender, race and time served. Candidates can, therefore, be new entrants to an organisation, trainees, apprentices or experienced employees regardless of the time served or their academic qualifications.

However, the methods of assessment will be unfamiliar so we would advise you that by starting with a small group you will have greater control. As your centre becomes more experienced you will be able to encourage access to NVQs/SVQs for a greater number of employees. By running a pilot study you will be able to reflect on and monitor what is happening. You should at this stage at least develop policies for recruiting candidates, even if you are not in a position to actually name people.

Start with a small group of volunteers and/or new recruits able to produce evidence that proves their competence. It would be sensible to include in your group those employees who are likely to persist and succeed. These people will then become champions for you in the future.

Identify the potential internal verifiers and assessors

The internal verifiers and assessors will be responsible for making sure that the NVQ/SVQ is a success.

The *assessors* are those individuals who actually assess candidates.

In order to maintain a consistent approach to assessment and ensure quality, all assessors must themselves be assessed to the national standards developed by the Training and Development Lead Body (TDLB). Therefore, assessors are required to achieve these TDLB units of competence:

- D32 Assessing candidate performance
- D33 Assessing candidates using diverse evidence.

Those assessors who are awarded unit D33, 'Assessing candidates using diverse evidence', may also provide a peripatetic assessment service to centres where there is no qualified assessor.

In addition to possessing units D32 and D33, assessors must also have relevant qualifications and/or adequate experience in the appropriate occupational area. After all, the assessor will be making judgements about a candidate's performance in relation to the relevant national standards.

Therefore, the role is not necessarily synonymous with that of a line manager, foreman or supervisor. Centres should encourage individuals like those for whom the NVQ/SVQ is designed also to become qualified assessors. The candidates' managers can also take an active part because they will know when the candidates are ready for assessment, and will be able to identify work activities that can be used for assessment.

The *internal verifiers* are those individuals who ensure the quality of assessment in an approved centre. They are responsible for advising assessors. They are the arbiters of assessment against the standards and are responsible for confirming an assessor's judgement that a candidate is competent. They will need to review a sample of assessments and organise meetings for assessors to help them review their role. In addition, internal verifiers are responsible for overseeing the administration of the scheme.

In order to maintain a consistent approach to verification and ensure quality, all internal verifiers must themselves be assessed to national standards. Therefore, all internal verifiers are required to achieve unit D34, 'Coordinating the assessment process'.

In addition to possessing unit D34, it is desirable for internal verifiers to hold relevant qualifications and/or to have adequate experience in the appropriate occupational area.

Internal verifiers should be senior members of staff. They must be capable of leading the team of assessors, making decisions about assessor performance, and redeploying assessors, should it be necessary.

The choice of assessors and internal verifiers is the responsibility of the centre. However, much will depend on:

- personal qualities
- experience
- credibility
- ability.

In addition to the internal verifiers a centre may decide to appoint a schemes administrator.

The *schemes administrator* maintains records of candidate performance, so that all records are kept up to date and reports are stored safely. In addition, the schemes administrator will liaise with the awarding body, register candidates and request certificates.

Centres are not obliged to appoint a schemes administrator. This function may be carried out by an internal verifier.

The schemes administrator may be required to:

- liaise with the external verifier, other departments as appropriate and the awarding body
- publicise the NVQ/SVQ
- send the application for approval to the awarding body
- keep records of external verifier visits
- register candidates with the awarding body
- co-ordinate assessments
- keep copies of all assessment records
- act as the centre's contact point.

It is difficult to provide definitive guidance on how many assessors and internal verifiers will be needed at a centre. However, a centre should appoint at least one of each. Centres will first need to determine the number of candidates. Then, bearing in mind how many times candidates will need to be assessed, and the amount of time assessors can devote to assessment, centres should be able to work out how many assessors and internal verifiers to appoint. As a rule of thumb, each assessor should ideally work with three candidates.

Establish a training plan for internal verifiers and assessors

Centres are free to train their internal verifiers and assessors as they see fit. However, any training programmes must prepare the internal verifiers and assessors to go forward for the TDLB awards. They must at the end of a training programme be able to carry out the assessment and verification process.

There are many organisations providing training in these areas. But make sure that the programmes do lead to assessment of the units and the award of recognised certificates. Internal verifiers and assessors should demonstrate that they are competent by running an assessment and verification system and by working with candidates practically. Therefore, it is unlikely that internal verifiers and assessors will receive their awards until an NVQ/SVQ is running at a centre with candidates. Internal verifiers and assessors will not be able to demonstrate competence unless they are actually working with candidates.

Identify work activities that can be used for assessment

Because candidates are assessed using work activities that they do every day, make a list of the work activities that have sufficient breadth and depth to match what is described in the standards.

This can often be the key to making sense of the units and elements contained in an NVQ/SVQ. Once people realise that work activities can be used to assess candidates, the system of assessment becomes less of a worry and the standards become a checklist and measure of performance.

Link standards into the needs of your business and your employees

Standards should be used to meet the needs of your business. The award of an NVQ/SVQ is the 'icing on the cake'. Your organisation should have a clear idea about where to expect improvements. Your aims might be to:

- reduce wastage
- improve profits
- reduce the risk of accidents
- improve communications
- improve efficiency

- create a more motivated, flexible, creative and responsible workforce
- improve understanding of how the business operates.

By identifying what you expect to gain at this stage, you will be able to measure whether these objectives have been achieved at a later date when the NVQ or SVQ is being operated.

Decide how to report to senior management

To maintain support from senior management, the results of the planning group and the fruit of their labours should be reported to and shared with senior management. Perhaps regular written reports could be submitted or presentations to senior management could be made.

Request a preliminary visit from the external verifier

Depending on the awarding body's arrangements, it might be possible to seek advice from the external verifier. If you have planned the preparation of your application for centre approval along the lines described above, you will have questions that need to be clarified. Any areas of concern can form the basis of a useful meeting with the external verifier before you actually put the finishing touches to your submission. If a preliminary visit is requested too early, then the external verifier will be teaching staff rather than helping them in practical ways. The external verifier is in a position to identify where gaps exist in the draft application for centre approval.

Visit other providers

Arrange to visit other organisations that have been approved to offer NVQs/SVQs. Ask staff how they developed the operation of their NVQ/SVQ. They will be able to advise you on how to avoid any pitfalls. Our experience is that people are more than willing to help new centres.

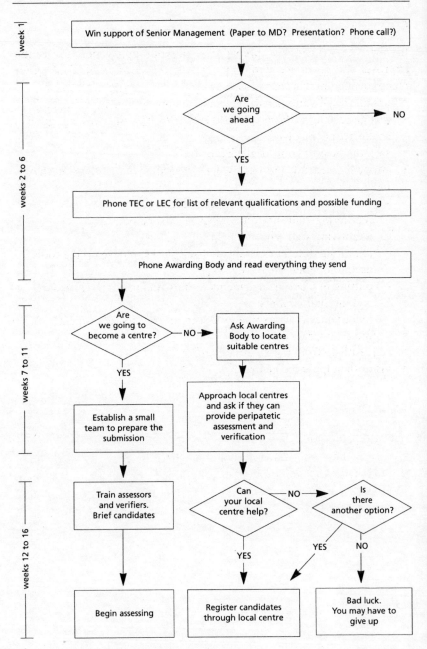

Figure 7.1 Critical path for getting started

RECOMMENDATIONS

In order to manage the preparation of your application for centre approval and introduce staff to the requirements of an NVQ/SVQ, we recommended in this chapter that you:

- use all the guidance available from the appropriate awarding body
- recognise at an early stage that the NVQ/SVQ will only be as good as the people involved
- seek the help of your local TEC or LEC
- adopt a systematic approach when preparing your submission that includes
  - gaining support from senior management
  - registering your interest with the awarding body
  - identifying staff who can help
  - allocating different members of staff tasks to develop the tools used to operate the NVQ/SVQ
  - putting in place arrangements to train and assess the assessors and internal verifiers
  - identifying work activities that can be used for assessment
- should set a target date
- request help from the external verifier
- visit other approved centres.

8 ASSESSING YOUR WORKFORCE

CHAPTER SUMMARY

This chapter discusses how the assessor and candidates can work together. We will describe how to approach an assessment, indicate what time will be needed, offer advice on using a variety of assessment techniques and describe how abilities needed by the employees for the workplace should be assessed.

THE FIRST STAGES OF IMPLEMENTATION

So you have prepared your application for centre approval to offer an NVQ/SVQ. It has been submitted to an awarding body. The external verifier has visited your organisation and has recommended that centre approval should be granted. The awarding body has granted your organisation approval to operate as an assessment centre for three years. Now what happens? If you are not careful, nothing!

As you move into the implementation stage, the internal verifiers, assessors and candidates will need support. For assessment to start, everyone concerned must understand what they are required to do. Candidates will need to be selected and briefed. Internal verifiers must work with the assessors to decide when assessments will take place. Assessment will need to begin. What follows is a description of how assessment is organised and what assessment methods can be used.

THE ASSESSMENT PROCESS

Candidates are responsible for producing evidence on how a real or simulated work activity was carried out. The assessors use all the evidence that is presented by the candidate to judge whether the national standards have been met. Therefore, assessors will need a variety of skills; such as the ability to communicate with candidates, organise assessments, observe and ask questions, and make assessment decisions. The relationship between the candidate and the assessor is very much a partnership, where together they agree how to prove that the standards are being met. But assessment will not happen automatically.

The candidates and assessors will need to organise assessments, as follows:

1 *Assessment planning.* Assessors and candidates agree which elements can be assessed, what evidence can be produced to meet the standards and how they will work together.
2 *Gathering and organising evidence.* Assessors and candidates produce different types of evidence to meet the standards in the elements being assessed.
3 *Judging evidence.* Assessors judge the evidence to make sure that it meets the standards.
4 *Reaching an assessment decision.* Assessors confirm that the evidence is sufficient to meet the standards.
5 *Recording the assessment decision.* Assessors record whether the candidate is competent. Further actions are agreed.

USING THE ASSESSMENT PROCESS

At each stage in the assessment process, expect the following to happen:
1 *Assessment planning*
  The assessor and candidate sit down together to plan how the candidate might prove that the standards are being met. When planning an assessment they should take the following steps:

  • Identify a recent, current or future work activity that would be used to satisfy the national standards.
    Questions:
    – What work activities does the candidate do?
    – Which of these work activities matches the elements in the standards?
    – Can one work activity provide evidence for more than one element?
  • Agree what types of evidence would be produced from doing the work activity.
    Question:
    – What different sorts of evidence would be produced from doing the work activity?
  • Agree how the evidence will be produced.
    Question:
    – How does the candidate plan to collect and generate the evidence?
  • Agree how assessment will be organised.

Questions:
- Are there areas of the candidate's work that the assessor will need to observe?
- Is there a need to check evidence supplied by the candidate with other people?
- When will the assessor judge the evidence?

2 *Gathering and organising evidence*

Providing that the types of evidence to be produced have been agreed at the assessment planning meeting, it should be quite straightforward for the candidate to collect and produce evidence. The method of producing the evidence will depend on whether a recent, current or future work activity has been chosen. The following time frame for producing evidence will apply:

- If the work activity was recently completed, the candidate will need to collect and gather the evidence retrospectively. This approach is often useful for employees who work on an annual cycle, where certain work activities take place at fixed periods throughout the year.
- For some people, particularly those who move jobs frequently, such as contractors, getting hold of recent evidence may be a problem. It may entail writing to former employers or clients and asking permission to use a piece of work done on their behalf as evidence of competence. Where the piece of work was confidential, permission could be refused. Unfortunately, not a lot can be done in such circumstances, except for the candidate to try and gather evidence when it is current and supplement it with reports of what was done rather than rely on original documents.
- If the work activity chosen for assessment is current and therefore ongoing, it will be relatively easy for the candidate to gather evidence. For example, a training officer may be running a course that is half-way through. The candidate will be able to collect the materials that have been prepared and generate more evidence such as course evaluations and plans to update the course in light of experience. The assessor may arrange to be present when the candidate is running the training course.
- If the work activity chosen for assessment is scheduled to take place in the future, the candidate will be able to collect and generate new evidence. For example, a systems design engineer

may be designing an operating procedure on how a particular piece of equipment must be used or maintained. The candidate would write a technical specification and test whether it works. All these records and documents would be produced as a result of carrying out the work activity. This approach lends itself more readily to employees who carry out normal or routine work activities. For example, a hairdresser may be assessed cutting and styling a customer's hair.

In summary, candidates can be assessed using work activities that have been completed, are currently ongoing or are going to be carried out in the future.

This flexibility allows candidates and assessors greater opportunity to identify a variety of work activities that can be used for assessment.

3 *Judging evidence*

The assessor and candidate sit down together to review the quality of the evidence against the standards. The evidence is used to judge whether the candidate has met the standards. The assessor checks that all the pieces of evidence are sufficient, authentic, relevant and current.

Although the responsibility for assessment rests with the assessor, the candidate should be encouraged to take an active part. Together they will discuss the work activity and the candidate will answer the assessor's questions designed to confirm competence.

4 *Reaching an assessment decision*

At the end of a review meeting, there are three possible outcomes:

- The candidate has met the standards and is therefore deemed competent.
  As a result the candidate can be awarded a unit certificate or an NVQ/SVQ.
- The candidate has not produced adequate evidence to meet the standards.
  As a result the candidate is requested to complete additional work or gather more evidence. A later date is agreed when the evidence will be reviewed a second time.
- The candidate has not met the standards. There are areas for improvement.

As a result the assessor recommends further action. This may include further training, further practice of skills or additional study by the candidate. However, when assessment is repeated at a later date, the evidence already produced by the candidate is still valuable and can be used again.

5   *Recording the assessment decision*
Depending on what assessment decision was made at stage four above, the assessment decision must be recorded. All the elements that were successfully met by the candidate should be signed off by the assessor and the internal verifier, who will need to be assured that the evidence proved competence as described in the standards.

METHODS OF ASSESSMENT

Awarding bodies have developed various methods of assessing and recording candidate performance. As systems have developed two common approaches have emerged. One approach is for assessors to use checklists to assess by observation and record what was observed. The other approach is to encourage candidates to produce all sorts of evidence that they use to demonstrate that they are meeting the national standards. Neither method is right nor wrong, in fact candidates usually can be assessed using a mixture of these assessment techniques.

Think, for example, of a surgical procedure. You can judge the operation by the subsequent health of a patient. The procedure involved to carry out the operation would be assessed using a checklist, which may include a list of items, such as the number of swabs required, so that none were left inside the patient. The assessor would observe the surgeon, ask questions and use evidence on how the operation was carried out to reach an assessment decision.

Observing candidates and using checklists

Work-based assessors use a checklist when they observe candidates carrying out a particular work activity. As the candidate satisfies what is described on the checklist, the assessor ticks it off from the list.

The checklist approach to assessment can be used when assessing the particular technical skills associated with a routine work activity, or where every step is crucial to the eventual outcome of the work activity. For example, a pilot engaged in pre-flight checks would be following a specific procedure.

Checklists should consist of a list of the sequential activities taken from an organisation's procedures, plus the criteria from the national standards to ensure that the right things were done in the right order and were done well.

The advantages of assessing by observation are that:

- each candidate is treated in the same way
- evidence is generated in front of the assessor
- it suits manual and procedural ways of working
- it is straightforward and undemanding of candidates.

In the first generation of NVQs/SVQs the checklist approach was used extensively.

Assessing by diverse evidence

As experience of running NVQs/SVQs has developed and lessons have been learned, another approach is not to observe candidates doing everything, but to encourage them to keep records on how the work activity was completed. These records prove that the candidates have met the standards contained within the elements being assessed. The assessor uses all the evidence presented by the candidate to reach an assessment decision.

This approach does mean that candidates need guidance on what types of report would make suitable and relevant evidence. It also requires candidates to be self-disciplined and motivated. The success of this approach lies in not producing more evidence than is necessary. Providing that assessors and candidates work in partnership at the assessment planning stage, where they identify work activities that can be used for assessment and agree what types of evidence can be generated naturally, the system of assessment can be simple and straightforward.

The knack is getting assessors and candidates to recognise that the documentation and record-keeping systems they would normally use can be used as acceptable evidence to demonstrate competence. This may also create the opportunity to update existing record-keeping systems used in your organisation. The advantages of using more diverse evidence are that:

- historical and recent evidence can be used
- evidence is from normal work rather than specially set assessments, and therefore more likely to be realistic
- assessors' time is not taken up by long periods of observation.

BRIEFING CANDIDATES

Much is made of training assessors and internal verifiers. But it is just as important to train and brief candidates. Candidates will need to understand the system of assessment. When asked, many centres report that candidates find generating evidence the most difficult activity.

We offer the following advice on what areas should be covered when briefing candidates.

- Explain that they will be assessed carrying out normal or routine work activities.
- Explain that they should identify which work activities can be used to assess their performance.
- Explain the role of the assessor and how together they work in partnership.
- Describe how all the different assessment techniques work.
- Describe how the assessor uses the evidence they produce to make judgements about their individual performance.
- Assure them that assessment is voluntary and that failure to take part will not affect their level of pay.
- Explain how they can use all the different opportunities to produce evidence.
- Explain how they can store their records and evidence in a portfolio.
- Describe how the candidate referral system is operated if they feel unfairly treated by an assessor.
- Describe how the NVQ/SVQ is linked into the needs of the business.
- Describe how the NVQ/SVQ should improve their own competence and individual performance.

Above all, introduce the candidates to the assessment system.

RECOMMENDATIONS

In order to assess the competence of your employees, we recommended in this chapter that you:

- make assessors and candidates aware that they work in partnership to carry out assessment in the workplace
- make time available for the assessor and candidate to plan, gather and judge evidence
- encourage the use of a variety of assessment techniques including diverse evidence
- encourage assessment of all skills and knowledge required by candidates.

9 BUILDING A PORTFOLIO

CHAPTER SUMMARY

In the previous chapter we described the system of assessment and how candidates are assessed. We recommended that a candidate should be assessed using a mixture of assessment techniques.

In this chapter we describe how candidates produce and store their evidence that shows how they have met the standards.

You will find examples of typical evidence that candidates can produce, guidance on where the evidence should be stored and advice on how candidates can use work activities to identify the evidence that they can collect and generate.

THE CANDIDATE'S RESPONSIBILITY

It is the candidate's responsibility to provide sufficient amounts of evidence to demonstrate that they are competent, which they store in a portfolio. The assessors cannot do this for the candidates, but the assessors will give advice on what evidence will be acceptable. The assessors' job is to use the evidence presented by the candidates to judge whether they have satisfied the standards.

Portfolios are personal to each candidate. Therefore, expect each candidate's portfolio to be different in terms of content and presentation. This can cause candidates concern if they are working towards the same NVQ/SVQ. Be prepared to assure candidates that this is expected and acceptable.

SOME BASIC QUESTIONS

- *What is a portfolio?* A portfolio is a collection of evidence to demonstrate that the candidate has satisfied the national standards and can be awarded an NVQ/SVQ or one or more unit certificates.
- *Why build a portfolio?* To satisfy assessors, internal verifiers, external verifiers, the awarding body, NCVQ and SCOTVEC that the national standards have been met.
- *Who builds a portfolio?* The candidate collects and produces evidence with guidance from the assessor. Contributions can be supplied by others with whom the candidate works. This is known as witness testimony.

- *When is evidence collected?* At appropriate times after an assessment plan has been agreed between the candidate and their assessor. Evidence should be generated naturally and be a result of carrying out a work activity.
- *Where is the portfolio stored?* The portfolio is the candidate's property, but experience tells us that if the candidate keeps the portfolio at home, it will not always be available. It is advisable to store the portfolio at the place of work, so that the candidate, the assessor, internal verifier and external verifier have access when necessary.

USING PORTFOLIOS

Portfolios can have two uses which are as follows:

An assessment portfolio. First and foremost the portfolio is used to prove that the candidate is competent. In this instance, a portfolio is used for assessment. To satisfy the assessor and the national standards, the challenge is to produce sufficient evidence to prove that the national standards have been met. All the evidence should be kept simple and be generated by carrying out a work activity.

A development portfolio. A development portfolio is used to describe in more detail what an employee does. This type of portfolio will contain more evidence than is required for the assessment of the national standards. For example, a development portfolio may include:

- a description of the organisation, including details on what the organisation does, serves or produces, how many people it employs, its geographical location and the nature of its business
- a description of how the organisation is structured and where the employee fits in, which can include details on who they report to and who they are responsible for
- a job description, which can describe what the employee is required to do and his or her responsibilities
- the employee's curriculum vitae, which includes details of educational and training records, qualifications, past achievements and areas of responsibility, and details of any successful projects or tasks carried out
- past appraisal forms
- lists of objectives and details on how they were achieved
- records of development plans, training needs and the results of any actions taken.

This type of portfolio can be used to introduce the employee to:

- internal people responsible for promotions or relocation of staff
- a prospective employer
- admission tutors responsible for recruiting students onto higher and further education courses.

Therefore this type of portfolio would help the employee's career development and progression. For the moment we will describe in more detail the assessment portfolio.

BUILDING AN ASSESSMENT PORTFOLIO

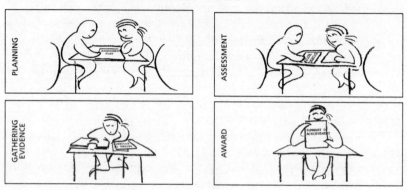

Figure 9.1 Recording progress and use of forms

An assessment portfolio should contain:

- records of what happened at each of the five stages in the assessment process
- items of evidence that the candidate has been able to collect and generate.

Recording progress

While we are sure that you will not want your candidates and assessors filling in loads of forms, you may find the following forms useful at each stage in the assessment process.

1 *Assessment planning.* During the planning meeting, the candidate can keep a record of what was agreed with the assessor:

- what evidence will be collected and generated from the work activity
- what methods of assessment the assessor will use, such as observation and questioning
- when the assessment will be carried out.

This record is known as an *assessment plan* and is used to:
- identify all the possible sources of evidence
- help the candidate through the work activity
- demonstrate that the system of assessment is being correctly conducted.

An example of an assessment plan is given on pages 101–2.

2   *Gathering and organising evidence.* At stage two, while candidates are generating and collecting evidence, they can keep a record which might include any of the following:
- Details of any paperwork used during the work activity such as drawings, diagrams, past job records, manufacturers' instructions, permits to work, handover sheets and completed signed off records. These sorts of records can be used as evidence to describe how the work activity was completed, but it is not necessary to photocopy everything the candidate used, referred to, completed or signed off. The Record of Evidence should state where these types of evidence are located.
- Witness testimony produced by other people.
- Records of answers to questions asked by the assessor.
- Descriptions of how a particular problem was solved.

An example of a Record of Evidence is given on page 102.

3   *Judging evidence.* At stage three, during the review meeting, the assessor can keep a record of what was discussed by completing an Evidence Review Report. This is a formal record between the candidate and assessor that records:
- what evidence has been collected and generated by the candidate and whether it met the standards and therefore whether it has been accepted by the assessor
- details of any work that the assessor observed the candidate carrying out
- any additional questions asked by the assessor and the answers given by the candidate
- details of any witness testimony accepted by the assessor
- requests from the assessor for further evidence because the

candidate has not fully met the national standards.

An example of an Evidence Review Report is given on page 103.

4 *Reaching an assessment decision.* At stage four, when the assessor decides that the candidate has met the standards in all the element or elements being assessed, the assessor should record the decision on an Assessment Record.

An example of an Assessment Record is given on page 104.

5 *Recording the assessment decision.* At stage five, when the assessor and candidate agree that the elements have been satisfied, the result should be recorded and signed off by completing a Candidate Summary of Achievement.

An example of a Candidate Summary of Achievement is given on page 104.

Different types of evidence

Evidence can be generated quite naturally provided that it is produced as a result of carrying out a normal work activity, but experience is showing us that there are two different types of evidence:

• performance evidence
• supplementary evidence.

So what is the difference between these different types of evidence? An effective way of explaining the differences is to recognise and understand how the different types of evidence are produced by candidates.

Performance evidence is generated as a direct result of carrying out a work activity. Opportunities to collect performance evidence will occur if the candidates:

• generate paperwork associated with the work activity, such as letters, memos, reports, or
• generate products, manufactured articles, repaired items of equipment or training materials.

Supplementary evidence is generated to support and explain further the performance evidence. It may often be produced following completion of a work activity. Opportunities to collect supplementary evidence will exist when candidates:

• keep records of answers to written and oral questions from the assessor using paper-based or audio systems
• complete simulated projects, case studies or assignments

- write personal reports on how they planned, prepared, carried out and reviewed the work activity
- requested testimony from an independent witness about their performance because the assessor was not present
- keep letters, memos and other records from people with whom they have worked.

Collecting evidence

As we do our jobs, we all keep records and complete work activities. With a little bit of extra effort, we can all produce evidence to demonstrate how we carried out an activity. The trick for assessors and candidates is not to miss opportunities to identify evidence. However, it is fair to point out here that candidates will be required to put in extra effort on top of their normal duties to produce and organise their evidence. But the evidence should be generated naturally as a result of completing a work activity.

When a candidate is generating and collecting evidence, they should bear in mind what the assessor will be looking for. The assessor will need to be satisfied that the evidence is:

- *sufficient*, by making sure that it meets what is described in the performance criteria and range
- *authentic*, by making sure that it is the work of the candidate; therefore, candidates are advised to include only items which they can substantiate as their own
- *relevant*, by making sure that it clearly relates to the work activity and the standards being assessed
- *current*, by making sure that it is recent enough to be proof of current rather than previous competence.

The list of items that can be counted as evidence can be endless. This can cause problems in that candidates can produce mountains of evidence. However, one way of cutting down the volume is to use one piece of evidence towards more than one element. Another is to agree at the planning meeting what evidence is expected.

Using witness testimony

Witness testimony can be supplied when the assessor is not available or when the candidate needs supplementary evidence about their performance. It should only be used when:

- it is provided by someone who is in a position to make valid

comment on a candidate's performance, eg supervisor, manager, colleague, customer or client
- it relates directly to the national standards in the elements being used for assessment
- it includes details of the witness.

Therefore each piece of witness testimony should include:
- a statement showing the candidate's relationship to the witness, eg supervisor, line manager, colleague, customer or client
- a description of the work activity carried out by the candidate
- details of how the work activity met the national standards
- a description of the context in which the work activity was observed.

The assessor must check with the witness that the testimony is authentic. This may mean contacting the witness directly. Therefore, the testimony should include the name, address and telephone number of the witness. It is advisable to submit the testimony on headed paper.

A PRACTICAL EXERCISE

In order to encourage the candidates to understand more about the assessment system and how they can keep records and produce evidence, we offer the following exercise to use with candidates:

EXERCISE ONE

Identify a routine work activity, then
- *describe the work activity*
- *list the skills required*
- *list the knowledge required*
- *list who else would be involved or affected.*

EXERCISE TWO

Match the work activity to one or more elements from the national standards. Read the national standards and list the types of evidence that you can generate by completing a copy of the assessment plan.

EXERCISE THREE

Categorise the types of evidence under the following headings:
- *Performance evidence*
- *Supplementary evidence.*

EXERCISE FOUR

Answer the following questions:
- *Is the evidence sufficient?*
- *Is the evidence authentic?*
- *Is the evidence relevant?*
- *Is the evidence current?*
- *How will you make sure that the evidence is an acceptable minimum?*
- *How will you make sure that you do not produce unnecessary evidence?*
- *What would you expect to happen at your assessment planning meeting with your assessor?*

CANDIDATE CHECKLIST FOR GENERATING EVIDENCE

You can generate and collect all sorts of evidence from a single work activity. Use this checklist to identify the different types of evidence that can be generated and collected.

1 IDENTIFY A WORK ACTIVITY
1.1 Have I identified a work activity that can be used for assessment?
1.2 Have I identified the skills needed?
1.3 Have I identified what I need to know?
1.4 Have I identified what is expected?
1.5 Have I identified who else will be involved?

2 USE THE STANDARDS
2.1 Have I matched the work activity to particular elements from the standards?
2.2 Have I read the evidence requirements?
2.3 Have I read the evidence specification?
2.4 Have I been able to identify the types of evidence needed to satisfy the evidence requirements and specifications?

3 IDENTIFY PERFORMANCE EVIDENCE
3.1 Have I identified the different types of performance evidence that can be generated?
3.2 Are there opportunities
* *to generate assessment plans?*
* *describe the work activity?*
* *collect assessment sheets and checklists used by the assessor?*
* *collect notes on feedback sessions?*
* *make reference to any materials such as documents, plans, checklists or manufacturers' instructions I will use during the work activity?*
* *record the assessment using photographs, audio or video equipment?*

3.3 Will I be producing:
* *designs for a new product or project?*
* *items that will be manufactured?*
* *modifications to existing equipment?*
* *a new administrative system?*
* *reports to management or customers?*
* *training materials?*
* *marketing or publicity materials?*

4 IDENTIFY SUPPLEMENTARY EVIDENCE
4.1 Have I identified the different types of supplementary evidence that can be generated?

4.2 Are there opportunities to record the answers to any questions I gave?

4.3 Are there opportunities to complete:
- *a project?*
- *a case study?*
- *an assignment?*

4.4 Are there opportunities to write personal reports?

4.5 Are there opportunities to seek witness reports from:
- *subordinates?*
- *peers?*
- *superiors?*
- *customers and clients?*

4.6 Are there opportunities to collect letters, memos and reports from customers?

4.7 Are there opportunities to keep a logbook or diary?

CHECK

5.1 Is the evidence I have generated and collected:
- *sufficient?*
- *authentic?*
- *relevant?*
- *current?*

Name

Signed   *Date*

ASSESSMENT PLAN

Candidate Name: *Number:*

The assessment plan relates to the following work activity:

IDENTIFY A WORK ACTIVITY:	*ELEMENTS:*
Record here the details of a work activity that can be used for assessment, ie describe the work activity	List the elements this work activity will meet

IDENTIFY YOUR EVIDENCE:	
Note here any evidence which is readily available and would normally be used	Note here any evidence that you can produce and collect, eg answers to questions, job plans, witness testimony, personal reports, fault-finding records

(continued overleaf)

101

ASSESSMENT PLAN (continued)

ORGANISE YOUR EVIDENCE:

Evidence for range
Note here how your evidence would meet the range specification. Is the work activity broad enough to meet the range specification?

Evidence for knowledge
Note here how your evidence would meet the knowledge specification. Is the work activity broad enough to meet the knowledge specification?

ORGANISE THE ASSESSMENT:

Record here how the assessor will assess you, eg When will the assessor observe you? When will the assessor ask you questions? What will you need to do in advance of carrying out the work activity?

Date of Assessment
Date of Review Meeting

Candidate (signature):   Date:

Assessor (signature):   Date:

CANDIDATE RECORD OF EVIDENCE

Candidate Name:
Candidate Number:
Elements Assessed:

The items of evidence listed below relate to the following work activity:

Evidence collected or generated List here the type of evidence you have used, collected or generated	Location of evidence Enter here where the evidence is kept	Relevance of evidence Enter here which elements and PCs this evidence satisfies		Assessor signature Assessor to sign here when evidence is accepted
		Element	PC	

EVIDENCE REVIEW REPORT

To be completed by the assessor

Candidate Name: *Number:*

Assessor Name: *Elements assessed:*

This review relates to the following work activity:

Details of work observed
Record here what you observed the candidate doing. Describe how the candidate met the standards. For example: Did the candidate have everything required to complete the work activity? Did the candidate deal with the unexpected? Did the candidate work to the job plan?

Details of evidence reviewed
Using the Candidate's Record of Evidence, record here how the evidence presented by the candidate is sufficient to meet the standards

Additional questions
I have asked the following additional questions to cover any gaps in the knowledge or range:

Details of further evidence required *Record here any gaps. List what further evidence is required*	*These further pieces of evidence are required for:*	
	Element	*PC*
Candidate (signature) *Assessor (signature)*	*Date:* *Date:*	

ASSESSMENT RECORD

Candidate name:
Candidate number:
Qualification and level:

Unit No.   Element No.

Date	Assessor	Proof of competence	Proof of knowledge and understanding

Element signed off (date)

CANDIDATE SUMMARY OF ACHIEVEMENT

Candidate name:
Candidate number:
Qualification and level:

Elements	Date element achieved	Units	Date Unit achieved	Signed	
				Candidate	Assessor

NVQ or SVQ certificate request approved by (internal verifier)
Unit certificate request approved by (internal verifier)

RECOMMENDATIONS

In order to help candidates record what happens during the assessment system and produce evidence to store in a portfolio, we recommended in this chapter that you:

- recognise that this is the candidate's responsibility
- recognise that each candidate's portfolio will be different in content and presentation
- recognise the difference between an assessment portfolio and a development portfolio
- recognise that candidates can produce both performance evidence and supplementary evidence
- encourage candidates and assessors to recognise the different opportunities that exist to produce evidence
- bear in mind that evidence must be sufficient, authentic, relevant and current
- make sure that the portfolio includes as much detail as possible to demonstrate how the candidate met the national standards.

10 IMPROVING THE DELIVERY OF THE NVQ/SVQ

CHAPTER SUMMARY

In this last chapter of Part Three, we will explain how to embed an NVQ/SVQ further into your organisation through a process of continuous improvement.

As you use the tools you have developed to support candidates, assessors and internal verifiers, they will need to be monitored and reviewed so you can identify which worked or failed. Armed with this information, you can update your systems for delivering the NVQ/SVQ to make them more efficient and effective.

We will describe how the external verification process can help you identify areas for improvement. We will offer practical advice on how to get the most out of monitoring visits by your external verifier. We offer guidance on how to keep your external verifier up to date with progress in between monitoring visits.

CONTINUOUS IMPROVEMENT

When he or she first visited you, the external verifier would have been looking for a commitment from your organisation to put in place systems for operating the NVQ/SVQ.

At this stage it is unreasonable for an external verifier and an awarding body to expect a centre to have in place a perfect system. But it is reasonable to expect the centre to look continuously for ways to improve how the NVQ/SVQ is operated.

A HIVE OF ACTIVITY

As a centre moves into the implementation stage, the activities below will have to be carried out.

* Candidates will need to be registered with the awarding body
* Candidates will need to be briefed about how the assessment system works
* Assessment documentation will need to be distributed to the candidates
* The assessment process will begin
* Internal verifiers and assessors will need to be trained, assessed and

awarded with their qualifications
- Management will need to be kept up to date with developments and receive progress reports
- The cycle of monitoring visits a year by the external verifier will begin
- The first successful candidates will be issued with unit certificates or NVQs/SVQs and celebrations will ensue.

Against this backdrop and hive of activity, staff at the centre and the external verifier will work together to develop further the tools that support the operation of the NVQ/SVQ. Both the staff and the external verifier should judge whether the tools that have been put in place are working and meeting the national criteria for centre approval and verification. Any systems used to operate the NVQ/SVQ should therefore be compared to the criteria. The external verifier monitors how a centre is progressing by making a centre approval visit and by making monitoring visits to the centre. Following each visit the external verifier issues a report that can include a list of actions that a centre should take to improve and update its systems for operating the NVQ/SVQ. Following the issue of reports, staff at the centre will be responsible for keeping the external verifier up to date with what is happening.

The external verifier will be able to identify areas for improvement, but from our experience the staff themselves will also want to make changes. It is essential that the staff at the centre keep the external verifier up to date with developments. One way of doing this is for the centre to issue regular reports to the external verifier.

THE SYSTEM OF VERIFICATION

As custodians of the criteria for centre approval and verification, the awarding bodies are free to run their own verification systems that allow staff at the centres to work constructively with their external verifier. However, the usual pattern is as follows.

- A centre seeks centre approval.
- The external verifier judges the submission against the centre approval and verification criteria.
- The external verifier visits the centre.
- The external verifier makes a decision over whether centre approval should be granted.
- The awarding body grants centre approval and sends the centre a copy of the centre approval report form.

- The centre acts on the actions contained in the centre approval report form.
- The external verifier makes two monitoring visits to the centre each year.
- Following each monitoring visit the external verifier issues monitoring visit reports.
- The centre acts on the actions contained in the monitoring visit reports.
- Between visits, the centre issues regular reports to the external verifier explaining progress and describing how the actions are being met.

At each stage in this process, staff at the centre and the external verifier will be identifying areas where further improvements can be made.

On the following pages you will find more detailed guidance on how staff at the centre and the external verifier can work together. We will describe what can be done to organise and carry out a successful monitoring visit and how centres can issue regular reports. Ideally, an external verifier should not police the system, but act as a judge by using all the available evidence compiled and assembled by the centre, to decide whether the operation of the NVQ/SVQ is meeting the criteria for centre approval and verification.

ORGANISING A MONITORING VISIT

The purpose of monitoring visits is to make sure that a centre continues to develop the system for operating its NVQs/SVQs. They are an essential part of an awarding body's quality assurance system. Centres should be continuously judging the operation of their NVQs/SVQs against the criteria for centre approval and verification.

What the external verifier is looking for

The external verifier will use the monitoring visit to:

- check if any actions requested in previous visit reports have been completed
- update and review action plans
- identify what still needs to be done or improved
- review whether work activities identified for assessment have the necessary breadth and depth to meet the standards
- discuss and clarify any problem areas
- review internal verifier and assessor performance

- review assessment documentation and candidate portfolios
- agree where further actions are necessary.

In addition, there may be particular areas that external verifiers will want to discuss, but they will probably refer back to their previous reports and any progress reports prepared by the centre. External verifiers may also be required to seek clarification on particular issues as requested by the awarding body. For example, the awarding body may be carrying out research into how centres are implementing their equal opportunities and access policies or how assessors are interpreting the performance criteria described in the standards.

Therefore, when the programme for the visit is being designed, it will need to take into account areas that the external verifier is particularly aiming to investigate.

Structuring a monitoring visit

We suggest that a programme for the monitoring visit should include.

- an initial meeting, where the external verifier goes over the aims of the visit and does a final check on which areas will be monitored during the visit
- visits to work areas and meetings with appropriate people, including managers, candidates, internal verifiers and assessors so that the monitoring process can be carried out
- a final meeting, where the external verifier provides the centre with feedback on the day's visit and discusses further action required.

Preparing the programme

The responsibility for designing the programme for the monitoring visit should lie with one person at the centre. This is normally the main contact person, usually the internal verifier, but in some cases this may be the scheme co-ordinator.

We recommend that a draft programme be prepared and sent to the external verifier for approval. At this stage the external verifiers can make sure that the programme will allow them to monitor areas of particular interest. Once the draft programme has been agreed, it should be circulated to people at the centre who will be involved in the visit.

The contact person at the centre is advised to:

- make arrangements for particular people to be available on the day to meet the external verifier
- assemble materials for the external verifier to review, such as

assessment documentation and examples of candidate portfolios
- prepare lists of any areas that are causing staff concern
- refer to previous visit reports issued by the external verifier and any progress reports prepared by the centre.

The mood of a monitoring visit

External verifiers aim to help centres develop their schemes; they do not police the system. Therefore, the mood during a monitoring visit should be one of cooperation, where staff at the centre and the external verifier work together to identify areas where the centre has been successful and resolve any areas of concern.

The visit itself

The external verifier will go through the programme for the day with the centre's contact and agree how to research particular areas of interest.

During the day the external verifier will be making sure that the operation of the NVQ/SVQ is developing to meet the criteria for centre approval and verification. The external verifier may need, for example, assurance that assessor meetings are taking place, or that candidates fully understand the centre's appeals procedure. The external verifier will want to see portfolios and meet candidates. Experience tells us that during a day's visit, external verifiers should meet a cross-section of candidates. External verifiers will want to meet assessors and check whether they have been issued with or are working towards their TDLB unit certificates. It may be appropriate to organise an assessors' meeting for the day of the monitoring visit. More candidates can be met if they join the external verifier for lunch. Portfolios could be assembled in one room, so that the external verifier can select which portfolios to see at random. The external verifier could meet more candidates at subsequent monitoring visits. The external verifiers should stipulate who they want to meet at a monitoring visit.

At the end of the day the centre's contact and the external verifier will review the day's programme to agree what will be written in the monitoring visit report. At this stage, further actions for the centre may be identified. A date for the next monitoring visit and the issue of the next progress report by the centre can be agreed. By doing this, the centre will not be surprised by any additional actions requested by the external verifier.

After a monitoring visit

Following a monitoring visit the external verifier will write a report of the visit. The report is sometimes sent to the awarding body who will forward a copy to the centre. The centre will prepare its next progress report for the external verifier.

ISSUING REGULAR CENTRE REPORTS

The purpose of issuing progress reports is to keep the external verifier up to date with what is happening at the centre. Armed with this information, external verifiers can offer centres additional guidance and advice, and plan for their next monitoring visit. In addition, external verifiers can normally only visit a centre once candidates have been registered with an awarding body. Therefore, for new centres, if there is a delay in registering candidates, it may be some time before the external verifier starts the cycle of monitoring visits, but they will need to know what arrangements are being made at the centre.

However, this can be overcome if centres register candidates with the awarding body within six months of receiving centre approval. Once candidates have been registered, the external verifier will normally make two monitoring visits to the centre each year.

Areas that can be included in a progress report include the following.

Meeting action plans

The external verifier will issue reports to the centre at the approval stage and after each monitoring visit. The reports may include action plans on areas where further developments are required. Therefore, centres will need to include in their progress reports details on how the actions have been met.

For example, the external verifier may have included an action point requesting that assessors be awarded with their D32 certificates. Therefore, the external verifier should be kept informed about whether certificates have been issued, or how the candidate assessors are progressing in terms of building their portfolios of evidence. Perhaps materials to brief candidates are being prepared. Perhaps the assessors are developing candidates' questions to assess the application of an underpinning knowledge. Perhaps a system for keeping candidate records is being developed. Perhaps the centre's equal opportunities and access policy is being monitored and evaluated. Details on these and any other actions agreed with the external verifier should be included in the progress report.

Completing assessments

Include a report on where assessments have taken place. This could include information on the work activities selected for assessment and details on which elements have been assessed.

Candidate registrations

Include details on the number of candidates who have been registered with the awarding body.

Changes in personnel

Include details on changes in personnel. Perhaps some staff have left or have been promoted. Perhaps new staff have become involved and are being trained and assessed to meet the relevant TDLB standards.

Additional information

We suggest that you could attach to the report any additional information to help the external verifier understand what is happening. Additional information could include, for example:

- the actual results of taking actions from previous reports, such as updated documents used for assessment, record keeping systems, questions developed to assess a candidate's underpinning knowledge practically in the workplace
- minutes of meetings with assessors
- reports prepared to keep management up to date with developments
- lists of questions raised by assessors and candidates on areas that have caused them concern
- materials used in briefing or training sessions
- materials used for assessment
- the candidate referral system.

In fact, any tools that have been developed to make the NVQ/SVQ work and support candidates can be used as additional items of information.

HEALTH WARNING

Centres who do not satisfy any actions requested by the external verifier normally run the risk of having centre approval withdrawn by the awarding body.

The development of quality systems and the practical tools to operate the NVQ/SVQ is seen as a continuous process. By preparing progress reports, centres will be able to satisfy the national criteria for centre approval and verification and ensure that assessment of candidates is fair.

CENTRE'S CHECKLIST FOR ISSUING REGULAR CENTRE REPORTS

- Have we agreed with the external verifier when progress reports will be issued?

- Have we decided what areas the progress report will include?
- Do we understand the actions requested on the external verifier's reports?
- Have we satisfied the actions listed on the external verifier's reports?
- Are we reporting progress on where assessments have taken place?
- Are we reporting on the quality and fairness of the assessment process?
- Have we informed the external verifier about candidate registrations?
- Have we kept the external verifier up to date with changes in personnel?
- Have we identified colleagues at the centre who can help complete the report?
- Have we attached additional information to the report?
- Have we included areas of concern for the external verifier to consider?
- Have we sent a copy of the report to the external verifier?

RECOMMENDATIONS

As part of your commitment to improving the operation of an NVQ/SVQ, we recommended in this chapter that you should:

- put in place methods of monitoring and reviewing systems used to deliver the NVQ/SVQ
- update systems for delivering the NVQ/SVQ based on your practical experience
- identify areas where changes may be necessary
- work in partnership with the external verifier to develop further your systems for delivering the NVQ/SVQ
- benchmark your performance against the national criteria for centre approval and verification
- prepare a draft programme for a monitoring visit
- involve as many appropriate people as possible during the visit
- issue regular centre reports to the external verifier, by providing details on
  - how the actions set by the external verifier are being met
  - assessment
  - candidate registrations
  - changes in personnel
  - the tools you are using to deliver the NVQ/SVQ such as record-keeping systems.

EPILOGUE: A CHANCE FOR REFLECTION

TEN YEARS OF DEVELOPMENT

It may come as a surprise to those new to the NVQ/SVQ world to know that ten years have passed since the first NVQs/SVQs were being prepared. The quiet revolution has, until recently, been largely unnoticed. In fact, until Professor Smithers brought it to the notice of several million viewers of the Channel Four 'Dispatches' programme, few were aware of the vast amounts of public money being spent on developments or on the impact that NVQs/SVQs were making on vocational and professional training and education in Britain.

The critics of the NVQ/SVQ movement have added to the debate and given us the opportunity to improve the quality of what we are doing. It is an appropriate time, therefore, to consider what has been achieved in the first ten years and to ask what can be achieved in the next ten years.

WHAT HAS BEEN ACHIEVED?

Awards made

Let's look at the numbers first. Around one million NVQs/SVQs will have been awarded by the end of 1995. That is equivalent to 4% of the working population. The target set by the government is for 50% of the working population (12.5 million people) to either have already been awarded NVQs or SVQs or to be working towards them. So, we are well short of this target.

Why? Both the CBI and the National Advisory Council for Education and Training Targets put it down to a lack of perceived relevance by employers. The NCVQ is being urged by both these bodies to:

- speed up the availability of SVQs/NVQs
- ensure that the standards and NVQs/SVQs are jargon-free and relevant to the needs of employers
- increase their marketing activities and, in particular, to work through the regional networks and with TECs to promote take up of NVQs/SVQs
- place greater emphasis on accrediting adults with prior learning.

Certainly a great deal has been achieved in developing the framework and in making qualifications available. But there has been little evidence of a co-ordinated and concerted effort to sell the benefits of standards and NVQs/SVQs and embed them into Britain's culture.

THE CHANGING ROLE OF EDUCATORS

Possibly the most radical change that has come about (and the most important, for it was a goal for the government in beginning this process), is the change in the role of educators. Formerly, educators designed curricula, and taught and examined students on the basis of what they believed students ought to know. There were a few colleges and universities who delivered programmes for specific employers, but not many. National provision, in the hands of awarding bodies such as City & Guilds, was based on syllabuses developed by working groups of practitioners and trainers. But no matter who was involved, the dominance of educators in the process led to provision that was almost always knowledge based, and more influenced by the ease, ethics and traditions of teaching than the priorities of employment.

On the other hand, the role of educators in a national standards programme is to design programmes which will deliver as an end product students who can do what is described by the standards. The standards are set by the priorities of employment. This has meant a radical change in role for educators.

The educators' role in shaping the standards

The national standards programme makes teachers into customers rather than suppliers of standards. Of course, they are not the only customers of standards but they are a significant group of customers. In this role they can help shape and determine the standards, not by making them education-led rather than employment-led, but by helping to make them understandable, teachable and learnable. In the early years, educators were kept at arm's length from standards developers and, as a consequence, the standards were less helpful to providers of training and learning than they might have been. The situation appears to be improving, and new partnerships appear to be developing at an earlier stage.

The educators' role in teaching and delivering competence

The second change in role for many educators is a shift from teaching principally knowledge and skills to teaching about the application of knowledge and skills in the workplace. In practical terms, this has meant that instead of concentrating on the theories, principles and facts in an area, teachers are now addressing the knowledge and understanding which underpins performance in an occupation. Instead of teaching specific skills that can be abstracted in a training room, teachers must now address the reality of the workplace environment. As a consequence, they have created:

- joint ventures with local employers

- more placements in industry during college and university programmes
- more realistic training content, exercises and simulations.

This is a good start, but what is required in future, if we are serious about developing a life long learning culture, is more partnerships between local organisations and training providers so that the training on offer meets the needs of businesses and employers by opening up opportunities for people to progress. To meet the needs of business, local training and education providers need to be flexible by organising the learning to fit in with the demands of the workplace.

For example, sending employees on day-release courses may not suit organisations who run their operations around shifts. North Trafford College, for example, has responded by running tutorials and teaching sessions at night time and at weekends, when employees are working their shifts; what's more, they run them at the trainees' place of work, not at the college.

THE EXPANSION OF TRAINING PROVISION

Although the take-up is still low, qualifications are now available for over 82% of the workforce. This coverage has led to an interesting discovery: that our education and training provision is inadequate. This is because national standards now cover areas of employment where traditionally people were not trained or educated. Therefore, more education and training provision will have to be developed to satisfy these people if they are to become qualified.

WHAT STILL NEEDS TO BE ACHIEVED?

A period of stability

The framework of occupational standards and qualifications in Britain currently covers 82% of people employed. During the development of the framework there were inevitable hiccups and teething problems. For some people, this led to a perception that:

- the whole of the national standards programme was just being tried out and could be scrapped at any time
- the situation was constantly changing and too difficult to keep up with.

As a result, some people stayed away from standards and NVQs/SVQs until things 'settled down'. Time has proved them wrong on the first count above; standards are definitely here to stay. The government's projected expenditure for the standards programme over the next two financial years is £11 million per year, only £1 million less than last year and there are no signs of abandoning the programme; rather, there are signs that NCVQ has been asked to develop it further.

On the second count, perhaps those organisations who steered clear of national standards until things settled down had a point. In waiting until the system has been refined and a period of relative stability begins, they have avoided getting their fingers burned. Some organisations adopted standards and NVQs/SVQs straight away. Some have stuck with it, helping to shape it, others dropped it, unwilling to be a test bed.

However, those who stayed away will have a lot of catching up to do compared to those who were pioneers. Besides, the argument about waiting until things have settled down is perhaps misguided. Even in a period of relative stability, the picture is changing. Standards are constantly being reviewed and updated; new ways of assessing knowledge and understanding are being explored; the concerns of the professions, as they become involved in shaping the philosophy and nature of the standards and qualifications, are being expressed. So, staying away is not necessarily the answer.

An attack on bureaucracy

There is no doubt that a system which aims to develop and measure the occupational competence of the entire British workforce is ambitious. The standards are thorough, detailed and many of them quite sophisticated. The assessment processes are demanding, rigorous and complex. Unfortunately, this has given rise to over-complicated and unnecessary bureaucratic support systems.

This need not be the case. With a little effort, even the most sophisticated system can be communicated in a simple, user-friendly way. Completing a tax return these days, for example, is almost a pleasurable experience. On the front page, the Inland Revenue lays out a Tax Payer's Charter, saying what they will do for you, how they will treat your tax affairs and what they need you to do in return. Such contractual statements between a provider and a customer of a service are becoming quite commonplace, but we haven't noticed any yet in the field of NVQ/SVQ delivery.

By referring continually to the standards, the base document if you like, we can cut down on the amount of additional paperwork, cross-referencing and additional layers of information.

By training assessors and verifiers well, we can help give them the confidence to make reasoned and sound judgements, based on a holistic appraisal of the evidence. Without that confidence, assessors are inclined to fall back onto vast reams of mechanistic paperwork to justify their judgements.

Better marketing

What also needs to happen now is for a comprehensive marketing strategy to be developed showing clearly the roles of the government, accrediting bodies, awarding bodies, TECs and LECs, and industry training organisations. Responsibility for co-ordinating the marketing effort, and accountability for its success needs to be located in NCVQ. The emphasis needs to shift from delivery of the qualifications to delivery of the training and development which lead to the qualifications. Perhaps as one way of achieving this, the government might set a target for the percentage of the workforce who know about the relevant national standards for their occupation and are working with them, being appraised against them and developed towards them by their employers.

Taking the plunge

It is worth considering that your employees may possibly have heard about NVQs/SVQs outside of work, perhaps through their children or friends. They may be wondering why your organisation is not getting involved. They may be tempted to interpret it as a sign of disinterest in them and their development. We will leave you with a few words from those who have taken the plunge.

> *'Our experience is that NVQs are flexible, relevant to our employees and bring bottom line benefits to the firm in terms of staff development of skills, competence and confidence.'*
>
> *Naomi Stanford, Training Manager, Price Waterhouse*

> *'NVQs are superb. They provide the key to unlock the potential of the workforce.'*
>
> *Alan Ward, Quality Manager, LGC Charlesworth Ltd*

> *'I think it has a tremendously positive influence – and I would really, really recommend people to look at the broader aspect of NVQs and not just the straight pay-back to business – because that is definitely there.'*
>
> *Tom Mahon, Divisional Manager, Glaxo-Wellcome*

So what are you waiting for?

SUGGESTED FURTHER READING

DFEE PUBLICATIONS

Research & Development Series
Competence & Assessment Series

Both series of reports are available from Roger Ellen, Pendragon Press, Papworth Everard, Cambridge, CB3 8RG

Credits Frameworks and Learning Outcomes Newsletter, edition 1

Guidance and Learning Autonomy Newsletter, edition 1

Work Based Learning Newsletter, edition 1

These three newsletters are available from Barbara Andrews, Higher Education for Capability, 20 Queen Square, Leeds, LS2 8AF

GOVERNMENT PAPERS

Working Together, Education and Training (1986), CMND 9823 ISBN 0101982305

Competitiveness: Helping Business to Win (1994), CMND 2563 ISBN 0101256329

Competitiveness: Forging Ahead (1995), CMND 2867 ISBN 0101286724

Available from HMSO Publications Centre, PO Box 276, London, SW8 5DT; tel: 0171 873 0011

NCVQ PUBLICATIONS

NVQ Monitor (regular update)

The NVQ Criteria and Guidance (February 1995)

The NCVQ Database

A statement by the NCVQ in response to *All Our Futures: Britain's Education Revolution*, a Channel 4 'Dispatches' programme on 15 December 1993 and associated report by the Centre of Education and Employment Research, University of Manchester

Available from NCVQ, 222 Euston Road, London, NW1 2BZ

SCOTVEC PUBLICATIONS

Accreditation Update

SVQ Criteria and Guidelines (February 1995)

Available from SCOTVEC, Hanover House, 24 Douglas Street, Glasgow, G2 7NQ; tel: Publications Section 0141 242 2168

CBI PUBLICATIONS

Quality Assessed, The CBI review of NVQs and SVQs (June 1994)

Thinking Ahead, 1994

Towards a Skills Revolution, Report of the Vocational Education and Training Task Force

Available from CBI, Centre Point, 103 New Oxford Street, London, WC1A 1DU

OTHER PUBLICATIONS

Mansfield, B and Matthews, D (1985) *Job Competence: A Description for Use in Vocational Education and Training,* FESC/ESF Core Skills Group Project, Bristol

Boyatzis, R E (1982) *The Competent Manager,* Wiley, New York

Burke, J W (1989) *Competency Based Education and Training,* Falmer Press, London

Constable, C J (1988) *Developing the Competent Manager in a UK Context,* A Report for the Manpower Services Commission, MSC, Sheffield

Woodruffe, C (1990) *Assessment Centres,* Institute of Personnel Management, IPM House, Camp Road, Wimbledon, SW19 4UX

Higher Education Quality Council (1995) *Vocational Qualifications and Standards in Focus.* Available from HEQC, 344–354 Gray's Inn Road, London, WC1X 8BP

Callender, C et al (1993) *National and Scottish Vocational Qualifications: Early Indications of Employers' Take-Up and Use,* IMS Report 259, Institute of Manpower Studies, Sussex

Eraut, M (1993) *Developing the Professions: Training, Quality and Accountability,* University of Sussex Professorial Lecture, Falmer Press

Hevey, D (1994) *What is Competence?* Occasional paper 1, Vocational Qualifications Centre, Milton Keynes, Open University

Smithers, A (1993) *All Our Futures: Britain's Education Revolution,*

'Dispatches', Channel Four, London

National Advisory Council for Education and Training Targets (July 1995) Report on the *Progress Towards the National Targets*. Available from Cambertown Ltd, Unit 8, Commercial Rd, Goldthorpe Industrial Estate, Goldthorpe, Nr Rotherham, S63 9BL

PERIODICALS

Competency, Industrial Relations Services, Eclipse Group Ltd, 18–20 Highbury Place, London, N5 1QP

Practical Training, Kay Davis Publishing, Shadingfield Hall, London Road, Shadingfield, Suffolk, NR34 8DE

NVQ/SVQ Focus and Care Standards, CS Publications, Unit 42, Price Street Business Centre, Price Street, Birkenhead, L41 4JQ

Personnel Today, Reed Business Publishing, Quadrant House, The Quadrant, Sutton, Surrey, SM2 5AS

People Management, Personnel Publications Ltd, 17 Britton Street, London, EC1M 5NQ

Human Resources, Martin Leach Publishing Ltd, Selous House, 5–12 Mandela Street, London, NW1 0DU

OTHER KOGAN PAGE TITLES

Lloyd, C and Cook, A (1993) *Implementing Standards of Competence*

Ollin, R and Tucker, J (1994) *The NVQ and GNVQ Assessor Handbook*

Fletcher, S (1994) *NVQs, Standards and Competence*, second edition

Brookes, J (1995) *Training Development and Competence*

Fletcher, S (1992) *Competence-Based Assessment Techniques*, Practical Trainer Series

Fletcher, S (1991) *Designing Competence-Based Training*, Practical Trainer Series

Fletcher, S (1993) *Quality and Competence*, Practical Trainer Series